CHILDHOOD EXPERIENCES OF SEPARATION AND DIVORCE
Reflections from young adults

Susan Kay-Flov

G000067692

P

First published in Great Britain in 2019 by

Policy Press
University of Bristol
1-9 Old Park Hill
Bristol
BS2 8BB
UK
t: +44 (0)117 954 5940
pp-info@bristol.ac.uk
www.policypress.co.uk

North America office:
Policy Press
c/o The University of Chicago Press
1427 East 60th Street
Chicago, IL 60637, USA
t: +1 773 702 7700
f: +1 773-702-9756
sales@press.uchicago.edu
www.press.uchicago.edu

© Policy Press 2019

British Library Cataloguing in Publication Data
A catalogue record for this book is available from the British Library

Library of Congress Cataloging-in-Publication Data
A catalog record for this book has been requested

ISBN 978-1-4473-3866-6 paperback
ISBN 978-1-4473-3865-9 hardcover
ISBN 978-1-4473-3868-0 ePub
ISBN 978-1-4473-3869-7 Mobi
ISBN 978-1-4473-3867-3 ePdf

Cover design by Robin Hawes
Front cover image: istock
Printed and bound in Great Britain by CMP, Poole
Policy Press uses environmentally responsible print partners

To my father, Jack,

husband, Gez,

and children, Laura, Emma and David

Contents

Figures and tables   vi

Acknowledgements   vii

one   Introduction   1

two   What is known about children's experience of parental separation and divorce?   7

three   The research study   41

four   Constructing a new framework for understanding children's accommodation of parental separation   67

five   Setting the context for the framework: emotions   87

six   Reactions   103

seven   Support   123

eight   Communication   141

nine   Conflict   153

ten   Future directions   167

References   181

Appendices

one   Case study for prompt simulation video (PSV)   189

two   Actors' script for prompt simulation video (PSV)   192

three   Online questionnaire   195

four   Respondent information: identifier number, current age, age at time of separation, gender and level of accommodation   199

five   Table of continua: respondents' positioning according to ID number   201

six   Framework for understanding children's accommodation of parental separation   202

Index   203

Figures and tables

Figures

2.1   The type of families in which children live: UK   9

3.1   Respondents' current age   56

3.2   Respondents' age at time of parental separation   57

3.3   Minimum time passed since respondents experienced parental separation   58

7.1   Respondents' sources of support during post-separation changes   126

7.2   People to whom respondents talked about their parents' separation   130

Tables

2.1   Number of couples with children divorcing in England and Wales and number of children affected (2009–2013)   10

2.2   Number of divorces in Northern Ireland and number of children affected (2010–2015)   12

2.3   Number of divorces and civil partnership dissolutions in Scotland (2011–2016)   13

4.1   Levels of accommodation: respondents who showed continuity across Continuum 1 and Continuum 2   77

4.2   Respondents who lacked continuity across Continuum 1 and Continuum 2   78

5.1   Characteristics of respondents in their early years at the time of separation   89

5.2   Characteristics of respondents in middle childhood at the time of separation   91

5.3   Characteristics of respondents in late childhood at the time of separation   93

5.4   Characteristics of respondents in early teenage years at the time of separation   96

5.5   Characteristics of respondents in late teenage years at the time of separation   99

Acknowledgements

My thanks go to the many people involved in this research study and those who supported the writing of this book. In particular I want to thank: the focus group members; those involved in constructing the PSV, the actors and Shaun Jeffers, the film maker; Pete Evans, the data manager; Chris Gillies who helped create the framework; Karen Brown and Dominic Cummings for many fruitful discussions; Peter Moss, Emeritus Professor at the Institute of Education, London, for supporting the initial idea for the book; Liverpool John Moores University for supporting my doctoral studies and the team at the Policy Press.

Most of all I want to thank the young adults who contributed to the study by recounting their experience, the bounds of confidentiality prevent me referring to you by name but you know who you are. I aimed to give 'voice' to your experience, I hope I have done justice to your accounts.

Then there are those who encouraged and supported me on the journey through the doctoral study to completion of this book; my thanks go to the 'Circle of Trust' for 'always being there'; to my children who 'endured' and then supported the experience as they matured; to my father for always believing in me and creating the opportunities he didn't have and finally to my husband, who has been 'my rock' throughout and without whom this would not have been possible.

ONE

Introduction

The effect of parental separation and divorce on children has been an area of considerable interest, leading to the creation of an extensive body of academic research over the last four decades. Many studies have focused on outcomes for children (see Rodgers and Pryor, 1998); more recent studies have sought to give 'voice' to children's experience (Dunn and Deater-Deckard, 2001; Butler et al, 2002; 2003; Wade and Smart, 2002; Flowerdew and Neale, 2003; Moxnes, 2003; Hogan et al, 2003; Smith et al, 2003; Smart, 2006; Bagshaw, 2007; Campbell, 2008; Halpenny et al, 2008; Menning, 2008; Maes et al, 2011). In these studies children's 'voices' have been mediated by parents who act as gatekeepers to their participation. Meanwhile the 'voices' of young adults on their childhood experience of parental separation and divorce have remained largely absent from this body of research, Fortin et al (2012) and more recently Du Plooy and Van Rensburg (2015), Brand et al (2017) and Morrison et al (2017) being exceptions. Their absence is curious as young adults appear particularly well placed to contribute to understandings of children's experience. In their case, separation occurred some time ago, allowing time for adjustment, and their transition to adulthood provides the opportunity to look back on their childhood experience in a different light. Giving 'voice' to their childhood experience provides valuable insight into what young adults saw as significant when their parents separated and post-separation changes were put in place, and how they accommodated the changes in their family life over time.

This book is based on a doctoral study (Kay-Flowers, 2014) which aimed to address this gap by providing the opportunity for young adults to talk about how they experienced their parents' separation and the post-separation changes that affected their lives as children. My motivation was to ensure young adults' 'voices' are heard in order to develop more nuanced understandings of children's experience, understandings which could be shared with academic audiences as well as practitioners to inform future work with children, young people and their families.

I had a personal motivation for undertaking the study, in my professional life I worked as a Family Court Advisor with the Children and Family Court Advisory Service (CAFCASS) working with children and families affected by parental separation, divorce or bereavement. Part of my role involved ascertaining children's 'wishes and feelings' about their family situation (Section 7 of Children Act 1989), these were then set within the wider context of the 'welfare checklist' in order to report the child's 'best interests' to the court. Representing children's wishes and feelings in written court reports made available to their parents presented challenges with children's voices often translated 'into a more acceptable register' in part to protect children, as practitioners feared parents 'might not like what children said about them' (James, 2007, 267). This study would give 'voice' to children's experience of parental separation without adult mediation.

The book reports findings from the qualitative research study which was conducted with young adults (aged 18 to 30 years). The study sought to learn about their lived experience, to understand aspects of experience which they considered important at the time and how they felt about their parents' separation and post-separation changes as they looked back now as young adults.

I worked with a group of young people to design the study and create the research tools. The internet was seen as the most suitable environment for young adults to talk openly about their personal experience of parental separation, with an online questionnaire a means of protecting their identity. It was questioned whether on its own this would generate sufficient interest to encourage participation. Focus group discussions suggested the construction of a short video clip about children's experience of parental separation would stimulate interest in the study and aid young adults' reflections: this became the way forward.

Working with a group of young people to co-create specific research tools for the study, we engaged in creating a bricolage: developing a fictionalised case study scenario which was dramatised and filmed to create a short video clip, which became known as the prompt simulation video (PSV), as well as an online questionnaire. The bricolage reflected the cumulative skills of the team. In the study, participants were asked to view the PSV before clicking on the link to the online questionnaire, in this way not only did the PSV act as a 'hook' to engage their interest but also as a prompt when considering their own childhood experiences of parental separation. The young people were involved in determining the process of data analysis, a process which involved scrutinising respondents' accounts to identify factors and experiences influencing their level of accommodation of parental separation over time. These were used to construct a new framework for understanding children's accommodation of parental separation and post-separation changes, making the findings readily accessible to different audiences.

As a qualitative study the aim was to learn about children's everyday lived experiences of parental separation and how young adults felt about it now, in order to understand and give 'voice' to their experience. Using respondents' own words, the 'voices' of young adults on their childhood experience of parental separation are reported faithfully in the book, the only alteration being to correct spellings so that mistakes do not serve as a distraction to the reader. 'Qualitative research tends to be based on the intensive study of a relatively small number of cases' and this study involved 34 respondents (Denscombe, 2017, 328). The study did not seek to test out previous research findings in relation to children's experience, nor to 'prove' or 'disprove' earlier theories, instead it sought to gain an in-depth understanding of individual experiences and to amplify their voices; therefore, this relatively small sample size was seen as sufficient for the task.

Throughout the book the term 'parental separation' is used to refer to parental 'separation' and 'divorce', the only time the term 'divorce' is used is when this is referred to specifically in the literature or in respondents' accounts.

Layout of the book

The book is organised in three parts: research, data analysis and construction of framework, and the concluding chapter.

Chapters One to Three: research

In Chapter One (Introduction) the reason for researching young adults' childhood experience of parental separation is explained and the nature of the study described. The process of working with young people to design the research and create a bricolage in which specific research tools were co-created is outlined and the layout of the book explained.

Chapter Two (What is known about children's experience of parental separation and divorce?) assesses the extent of divorce and parental separation and the number of children affected across the United Kingdom. Differences in the way the Home Nations – England, Wales, Scotland and Northern Ireland – collect such information and the information they collect means that the picture is incomplete. The chapter goes on to explain the reasons for focusing on children's 'voice' and reviews those research studies which have given 'voice' to their experience of parental separation and divorce. Findings are reported according to the themes emerging from the review which were: parents' communication with children; children's involvement in decision-making; continuity in post-separation arrangements; parental support for children; children's experience of parental conflict; children's experience of post-separation family transitions and looking back on childhood experiences of parental separation.

The nature of the study, focusing on children's everyday lived experience of parental separation and the involvement of young people in the research design, construction of the research tools and analysis of the data are described in Chapter Three (The research study). Adopting a participatory approach, I worked *with* young people to determine the research design which involved the creation of specific research tools to investigate young adults' experience. As the researcher I worked as a bricoleur with young people to co-create the PSV, the short video clip of a fictionalised case study of children's experiences of parental separation, and an online questionnaire. The stages and processes involved in creating this bricolage are explained. The chapter goes on to describe the process of data analysis which involved categorising responses to the question which asked how respondents felt about their parents' separation now; this was done according to the level of satisfaction (Contiuum 1) and the level of acceptance (Continuum 2) expressed. Where these coincided, a respondent's level of accommodation of parental separation – high, medium or low – could be established. This became the central category for further analysis, enabling aspects of their experience and factors influencing levels of accommodation to be identified. The chapter concludes with reflections on the strengths and weaknesses of the research methodology and limitations of the study.

Chapters Four to Nine: data analysis and construction of framework

In the second part of the book Chapter Four explains how analysis of the data led to construction of a new framework for understanding children's accommodation of parental separation and post-separation changes, based on consistent themes emerging from their experience. The themes reflected clusters of experience influencing individual levels of accommodation of parental separation over time and were used to create the framework. The themes are examined in detail in a series of discrete chapters, focusing on Reactions (Chapter Six), Support (Chapter Seven), Communication (Chapter Eight) and Conflict (Chapter Nine).

Chapter Four (Constructing a new framework for understanding children's accommodation of parental separation) shows how individual responses were positioned on Continuum 1 and Continuum 2 and the continua used as a framework for thematic analysis of the data. Experiences tended to be clustered according to whether they showed a high, medium or low level of accommodation of parental separation, the clustering of experiences allowed a new framework for understanding children's accommodation of parental separation to be constructed. The chapter outlines the new framework and explains how it can be interpreted to create a deeper understanding of factors and experiences influencing a child's accommodation of parental separation.

The context for understanding children's experiences is set in Chapter Five (Setting the context for the framework: emotions) where children's initial emotional responses on finding out that their parents were separating are described. Children's age at the time of separation influenced their awareness and ability to understand what was happening in their family and to make sense of events, therefore responses are reported according to their age at the time of parental separation.

The next four chapters examine the factors and experiences influencing children's accommodation of parental separation outlined in the framework, they provide a detailed understanding of individual children's experiences and how they accommodated their parents' separation. Each chapter starts with a case study of one respondent's account.

Children's reactions to their parents' separation and the changes it brought to their lives are described in Chapter Six (Reactions), which also takes account of other family members' responses, particularly those of parents and siblings, since these often had an impact on individual children's experiences. Children's reactions are reported according to their age at the time of separation, enabling the reader to build on knowledge of their emotional responses gained in Chapter Five. It concludes with discussion of how children's reactions and other family members' responses influenced their level of accommodation of parental separation.

The support available to children at the time of parental separation and opportunities they had to talk to other people about their parents' separation are identified in Chapter Seven (Support). Their experiences are examined in relation to their impact on children's accommodation of parental separation. Consideration is also given to the opportunities which respondents would have liked to have been available, in terms of who they may have chosen to talk to outside the family about their parents' separation.

The quality of parental communication during parental separation and in post-separation decision-making, is the focus of Chapter Eight (Communication). In this chapter, the impact of children being informed of their parents' separation in advance and feeling that their views were taken into consideration in decision-making about post-separation changes are examined in relation to their level of accommodation.

Chapter Nine (Conflict) describes respondents' experiences of parental conflict and examines how these had an impact on their accommodation of parental separation. It describes the negative impact of parental conflict on children's social and emotional wellbeing and their feelings of relief when conflict ended following parental separation, this was reflected in higher levels of accommodation. These experiences were in marked contrast to those young adults who continued to experience parental conflict and showed a low level of accommodation. The positive role of family support in enabling children to adjust was highlighted in some accounts.

Chapter Ten: future directions

Chapter Ten (Future directions) represents the third and final part of the book. The chapter explores ways in which practitioners might use the framework to understand children's accommodation of parental separation and support their work with children. Set within the context of what young adults had to say about who they might like to have talked to about their parents' separation and what information would have been useful to them at the time, consideration is given to who is best placed to support children in educational settings such as schools and universities and how they might best be supported. Attention is also given to how the framework might be used in work with parents to encourage a deeper understanding of how their actions, responses and decisions about arrangements can promote a higher level of accommodation of parental separation for their children. It concludes by highlighting the need for professional dialogue with practitioners to explore these avenues.

TWO

What is known about children's experience of parental separation and divorce?

This chapter starts by describing the different types of families in the United Kingdom (UK) and goes on to explain some of the legislation governing marriage, civil partnerships and divorce. The UK comprises four home nations – England, Wales, Scotland and Northern Ireland – and there are legislative differences between them. Using data collected in each of the home nations the extent of divorce and civil partnership dissolution can be established and the number of children affected ascertained in England, Wales and Northern Ireland. Differences in the way the Scottish government collects data means that this information is not available in relation to Scottish children.

Legal processes involved in entering into marriage or civil partnership, and the ending of such relationships, means that the number of people affected can be established with some certainty, unlike couples who choose to live together informally as cohabiting couples. Office for National Statistics (ONS) statistics estimate the number of children who live in cohabiting couple families in the UK but the number affected by separation cannot be determined because such information is not collected.

The second part of the chapter explains the reasons for focusing on children's 'voice' and why this is important. Drawing on research from around the world, it reviews studies that articulate children's 'voice' in relation to their everyday experience of parental separation and divorce and identifies common themes emerging from the findings. The studies are identified and details relating to the age of children, size of sample and geographic location of the study, are provided.

The third part of the chapter describes what children said about their experience of parental separation.

Family types in the UK

The population of the four home nations of the UK is estimated to have been 65,648,054 people in mid-2016, which is the highest it has ever been (ONS, 2017a). Most of the people living in the UK live in

England, which has a population of just over 55,200,000; 3,100,000 live in Wales, about 5,400,000 live in Scotland and over 1,800,000 live in Northern Ireland. Growth in the UK population is reflected in an increased number of families living in the UK, from 16.6 million in 1996 to 19.0 million in 2017 (ONS, 2017b).

In 2017 there were 14 million dependent children living in the UK, dependent children are defined as those aged under 16 or aged 16–18 in full-time education (ONS, 2017b). They were most likely to live in married couple families and 64 per cent of children (almost 9 million) lived in such families (see Figure 2.1 below). The term 'married couple family' includes both opposite and same-sex couples and those who have married more than once (ONS, 2017b). The number of married couple families has remained relatively stable, growing only 0.3 per cent in the last two decades (ONS, 2017b).The fastest growing family type has been the cohabiting couple family, increasing from 1.5 million families in 1996 to 3.3 million families in 2017, with the proportion of dependent children living in such families more than doubling from 7 per cent in 1996 to 15 per cent in 2017 (ONS, 2017b). Just over 2 million children lived in such families in the UK in 2017 (see Figure 2.1 below) (ONS, 2017c). The term 'cohabiting couple family' includes both opposite and same-sex couples, less than 1 per cent of children were found to live in civil partner couple families (ONS, 2017b).

The number of lone parent families has also increased over the last two decades to 2.8 million in 2017, accounting for 21 per cent of dependent children, and are usually led by females (see Figure 2.1 below) (ONS, 2017b).

Marriage, civil partnership and divorce in the UK

Since marriage and civil partnerships are governed by legislation, it is possible to establish the number of people marrying, forming civil partnerships, divorcing and dissolving civil partnerships in the UK. The Civil Partnership Act 2004 came into force across the UK in December 2005, enabling same-sex couples to have their relationship legally recognised and providing access to many of the rights commonly associated with marriage. At the time of writing the UK government proposes to legislate to allow all couples in England and Wales, regardless of gender, to have a Civil partnership. This is in response to a Supreme Court ruling widely reported on 2 October 2018. There are some differences in the law relating to same-sex marriage which will be explained in the following sections on each of the home nations.

Figure 2.1: The type of families in which children live: UK

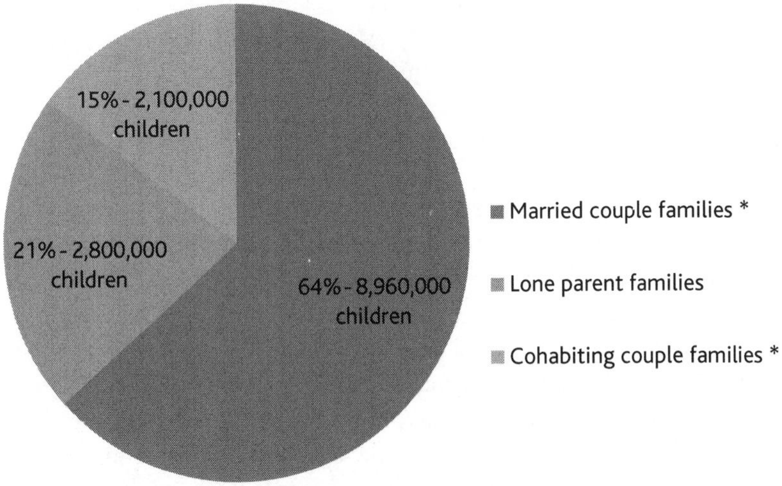

15% - 2,100,000 children

21% - 2,800,000 children

64% - 8,960,000 children

- Married couple families *
- Lone parent families
- Cohabiting couple families *

Notes: * includes same sex and opposite sex relationships. Number of children = 14.0 million.

Source: Statistics taken from ONS (2017b)

Divorce statistics show those married couples who have separated and obtained a decree absolute, representing the final legal stage in the dissolution of a marriage; a similar process is undertaken in relation to the dissolution of a civil partnership. The next part of the chapter outlines the incidence of divorce and civil partnership dissolution in each of the home nations and where possible the number of children affected. The statistics do not show those married couples or civil partners who have separated but not divorced or applied for dissolution of their partnership, meaning only a partial picture of children's experience of parental separation is available.

Parental separation and divorce in the UK

England and Wales

Divorce in England and Wales is governed by four main pieces of legislation: the Divorce Reform Act 1969, the Matrimonial and Family Proceedings Act 1984, the Marriage (Same Sex Couples) Act 2013 and the Children and Families Act 2014. Marriage between same-sex couples was legalised in England and Wales in 2013 and the first same-sex marriages took place in March 2014.

Since the introduction of the Divorce Reform Act 1969 there has been an increase in the percentage of marriages ending in divorce in England and Wales. Office for National Statistics (ONS, 2017d) figures show 22 per cent of marriages entered into in 1970 ended by the fifteenth wedding anniversary, whereas 33 per cent of marriages entered into in 1995 ended by this time, divorce being most likely to occur within the first 10 years of marriage. More recent figures show an overall decrease in the incidence of divorce among those marrying since 2000 (ONS, 2017d). Introduction of the Marriage (Same Sex Couples) Act 2013, means that divorce among same-sex couples is now possible, 112 divorces of same-sex couples were recorded in 2016, over three-quarters (78 per cent) were among female couples (ONS, 2017d).

Legislative changes brought about by the Children and Families Act 2014 means that married couples seeking a divorce are no longer required to disclose details about their children and so statistics relating to the number of children affected by divorce have not been collected since 2015 (ONS, 2017d). To assess the number of children in England and Wales affected by divorce, reference needs to be made to earlier statistics which were last collected in 2013 (ONS, 2015). Information relating to the number of couples with children divorcing, the number of children aged under 16 and those aged 16 and over experiencing their parents' divorce between 2009 and 2013 can be found in Table 2.1 (ONS, 2015). The average number of children per couple and their age is also shown. The highest recorded number of couples divorcing

Table 2.1: Number of couples with children divorcing in England and Wales and number of children affected (2009–2013)

Year	Number of couples with children divorcing	Number of children aged under 16	Number of children aged 16 or over	Average number of children per couple aged under 16	Average number of children per couple aged over 16
2013	55,323	94,864	14,841	1.71	0.27
2012	57,139	99,822	16,185	1.75	0.28
2011	57,219	100,760	17,619	1.76	0.31
2010	59,309	104,364	18,936	1.76	0.32
2009	56,695	99,543	19,068	1.76	0.34
1993 – highest number	94,915	175,961	20,573	1.85	0.22
Total number from 2009–2013	285,685	499,353	86,649	N/A	N/A

Source: Statistics drawn from ONS, 2015

and the highest number of children aged under 16 affected by divorce was recorded in 1993, this data is included in Table 2.1 for the purposes of comparison. In that year 94,915 couples divorced, affecting 175,961 children under 16 and 20,573 children aged 16 and over, the average number of children per couple was 1.85 and 0.22 respectively.

Since 2010, when almost 60,000 couples with children divorced, affecting around 104,000 children under the age of 16 and almost 19,000 aged 16 or over, the number of couples divorcing and the number of children affected has decreased year on year. The table shows that in 2013, 55,323 couples with children divorced and 94,864 children under 16 as well as 14,841 children aged 16 or over experienced their parents' divorce; this was the lowest number of couples divorcing and the lowest number of children affected during this five-year period. The average number of children per couple has also decreased during this time from 1.76 children aged under 16 in 2010 to 1.71 in 2013 and 0.32 children aged over 16 in 2010 to 0.27 in 2013.

Overall, in the five years leading up to and including 2013, 285,685 couples with children divorced in England and Wales, just under half a million (499,353) children under the age of 16 were affected alongside 86,649) children aged 16 and over, meaning a total of 586,002 children were affected by their parents' divorce.

Northern Ireland

Statistics produced by the Northern Ireland Statistics and Research Agency (NISRA) show the number of married couples divorcing and the number of children affected by divorce each year in Northern Ireland. They show a steady increase in the number of couples seeking divorce in the 1980s and 1990s with the number peaking at the onset of the 'Great Recession' in 2007 when 2,913 couples divorced (NISRA, 2015). Since then the number has reduced, as can be seen in Table 2.2, which shows the number of divorces and number of children/ stepchildren aged under 16, aged 16–18 and aged over 18, affected by divorce in Northern Ireland from 2010 to 2015 (NISRA, 2011; 2012; 2013; 2014; 2015; 2016).

NISRA recorded children's ages according to the categories used by the Registrar General as 'under 18' or 'aged 18 and over'. Since 2014 data has been recorded according to whether a child is aged 'under 16', '16–18' or '18 and over' these changes are reflected in Table 2.2.

Over the last six years the number of divorces in Northern Ireland has varied from a high of 2,600 in 2010 to a low of 2,343 in 2011, figures have remained relatively stable with an average of 2,434 divorces each year. The number of children/stepchildren aged under 18 experiencing their parents' divorce varied from a high of 2,709 in 2010 to a low of 2,200 in 2015, an average of 1,768 children have been affected each year. More recent figures show the number of children and stepchildren aged 16–18 years at the time of parental divorce; there were 700 children in this age category in 2014 and 400 in 2015.

The largest number of children/stepchildren aged 18 and over experiencing their parents' divorce was recorded in 2015 when 2,000 young adults experienced this event. The lowest number of young adults experiencing parental separation (1,600) was recorded in 2011. Overall an average of 1,768 children aged 18 and over experienced their parents' separation each year.

NISRA statistics show that in the six-year period up to and including 2015, just under 15,000 (14,849) children and stepchildren aged under 18 experienced their parents' divorce alongside 10,605 children and stepchildren aged 18 and over, meaning a total of 25,454 children were affected by their parents' divorce. This number does not include children of same-sex couples because same-sex marriage is not recognised in Northern Ireland.

There have been 1,026 civil partnerships in Northern Ireland since the Civil Partnership Act 2004 came into force in 2005 (NISRA, 2012).

Table 2.2: Number of divorces in Northern Ireland and number of children affected (2010–2015)

Year	Number of divorces	Number of children/ stepchildren age under 16	Number of children/ stepchildren age 16–18 years	Number of children/ stepchildren age 18 and over
Average over last six years (2010–2015)	2434	2475 under 18 and 1768 aged 18 and over		
2015	2360	1800	400	2000
2014	2455	1900	700	1700
2013	2403	2400 under 18 and 1700 aged 18 and over		
2012	2444	2540 under 18 and 1790 aged 18 and over		
2011	2343	2400 under 18 and 1600 aged 18 and over		
2010	2600	2709 under 18 and 1815 aged 18 and over		
Total number from 2010 to 2015	14,605	14,849 children/stepchildren aged under 18 and 10,605 children/stepchildren aged 18 = 25,454 children		

Sources: NISRA, 2011, 2012, 2013, 2014, 2015, 2016

The first partnership dissolutions were registered in 2010 when there were three (NISRA, 2011); since then there has been a small increase each year with 11 recorded in 2014, female couples have been more likely to seek dissolution of a civil partnership (NISRA, 2016).

Scotland

Scottish Government statistics show the number of divorces and civil partnership dissolutions taking place in Scotland, but do not record the number of children affected (Scottish Government, 2017). The number of divorces and civil partnership dissolutions in Scotland in the five-year period from 2011 to 2016 can be seen in Table 2.3 which shows a year on year reduction from 9,903 in 2011–2012 to 8,875 in 2015–2016 and is a significant reduction since 1985, when 13,300 divorces took place (Scottish Government, 2017).

Same-sex marriage was legalised in Scotland by the Marriage and Civil Partnership (Scotland) Act 2014, and the first ceremonies took place in December of that year. Scottish legislation allows couples in civil partnerships to change their relationship into a marriage (Scottish Government, 2017).

Table 2.3: Number of divorces and civil partnership dissolutions in Scotland (2011–2016)

Year	Number of divorces and civil partnership dissolutions
2015–16	8875
2014–15	9030
2013–14	9626
2012–13	9694
2011–12	9903

Source: Scottish Government, 2017

Cohabitation figures

Over the last two decades there has been an increasing trend for couples to cohabit rather than marry, or to cohabit before marriage in the UK and over 2 million children are estimated to live in cohabiting couple families, accounting for 15 per cent of dependent children (see Table 2.1) (ONS, 2017b). The informal nature of cohabitation presents difficulty in obtaining accurate figures about the number of children living in this type of family and the extent of relationship breakdown.

The number of children affected by the separation of cohabiting parents cannot be determined because such information is not collected by the Office for National Statistics (ONS, 2017b). Some insight can be gleaned from analysis of census data relating to England and Wales only and is reported in the following section.

England and Wales

Collected every 10 years from every household, census data relating to England and Wales only showed, in 2011, 1.1 million (9 per cent) dependent children lived in a stepfamily, of these 689,000 children lived in married couple stepfamilies and 418,000 lived in cohabiting couple stepfamilies. This indicates that, of the 1.7 million children living in cohabiting couple families, nearly a quarter (24 per cent) lived in stepfamilies (ONS, 2017b). However, caution needs to be exercised when using these figures because they may include natural children of the couple as well as children from either or both partners' previous relationships.

Further insight can be gained from census data relating to dependent children with a parental second address, that is, children who share their time between two different parental addresses (ONS, 2014). This question was asked for the first time in the 2011 census and while not limited to children whose parents cohabit, it showed 386,000 (3.2 per cent) of dependent children in England and Wales had a second parental address. They were most likely to have a second address in the same local authority as their usual residence but 4 per cent had a second address outside the UK, indicating contact with one parent involved navigating geographical distance (ONS, 2014).

The picture relating to the number of children affected by parental separation among cohabiting couple families in England and Wales remains incomplete and there are clear gaps in our knowledge in relation to Scotland and Northern Ireland.

Number of children affected by divorce across the UK

From available statistics it is known that 628,786 children in three of the four home nations experienced their parents' divorce during the period 2009 to 2015. It is unknown how many Scottish children experience their parents' divorce.

Previous estimates have suggested that one in three children in the UK will experience their parents' separation or divorce before the age of 16, while this cannot be established with certainty, it provides an indication of the extent of the experience among children (Layard and Dunn, 2009; Fortin et al, 2012).

The chapter now turns attention to children's experience of parental separation and the importance of their 'voice' in understanding what they have to say about the experience.

Why the focus on children's 'voice'?

Children's experience of parental separation has been subject to intense scrutiny, extensive research has been conducted on the effects of parental separation, outcomes for children who have experienced separation in childhood, the experience of living in stepfamilies and their involvement in decision-making about post-separation arrangements. Their views on the experience, however, have been less well documented and the 'voice' of young adults looking back on their childhood experience of parental separation has been largely absent from the body of research. This study sought to address the gap by focusing on how children experienced their parents' separation in their everyday lives, what it meant to them, the changes it brought and how they viewed the experience as they looked back as young adults, thereby giving 'voice' to their childhood experiences of parental separation.

Giving 'voice' to children's experience means seeing children as 'competent social actors' with agency in their own lives (James, 2007), engaging with the perspectives they provide about their social world (Smart, 2003; James, 2007) and listening in order to ascertain their understanding and the meaning they give to their experience (Hadfield and Haw, 2001). 'Voice' links closely to participation and empowerment and is an approach used to research groups of individuals whose views have often been overlooked or excluded (Hadfield and Haw, 2001). In the case of parental separation, children's views of their experience are mediated by adults (parents) who act as gatekeepers to their participation and control whether their voices are heard (Birnbaum and Saini, 2012a). The purpose of this study was to ensure that children's voices are heard by providing the opportunity for young adults to speak for themselves about their childhood experience.

Accessing children's 'voice' is not without its challenges, researchers need to develop new approaches which are attractive to children to engage their interest and seek appropriate ways to listen to what children have to say about their experiences (Hadfield and Haw, 2001). Then there is the issue of interpreting and representing children's voices, choosing what and how to present the findings, selecting phrases to represent their views, decisions raising theoretical and conceptual difficulties around authenticity of their voices (Campbell, 2008; Spyrou, 2011). Even when represented faithfully, children may 'find their voices silenced, suppressed, or ignored' because adults do not see them as mature and treat their views with suspicion (James, 2007, 261), because professionals struggle with the tension between young people having 'unique insights' and their lack of 'experience' or 'maturity' (Hadfield and Haw, 2001, 494) or because the researcher moves from the child's frame of reference to the adult researcher's frame of reference imposing their own meaning on the data collected (Campbell, 2008; Spyrou, 2011).

Recent attempts to address power differentials inherent in the researcher/researched relationship have involved researching '*with* children rather than *on* children' with some researchers using children as co-researchers. Whether such research 'necessarily represents a more accurate or authentic account of children's issues' or sufficiently addresses adult–child (researcher/researched) power relations has been questioned (James, 2007, 263; Spyrou, 2011). These issues are considered in Chapter Three (The research study) when looking at the process of data analysis in this study.

Relevant studies

Focusing on young adults' childhood experiences of parental separation to give 'voice' to their everyday lived experience of parental separation, it was important to understand what was already known about their experience. Therefore, a review of relevant studies focusing on children and young people's everyday experience of parental separation and divorce was undertaken, all of the following criteria were a requirement for a study to be included in the review:

- the research was conducted with children and/or young adults who had experienced parental separation or divorce in childhood;
- it investigated their own reported experiences of parental separation or divorce;
- it focused on their everyday experience.

Studies addressing the gap in research on young adults' childhood experience of parental separation published after this study was undertaken, such as Du Plooy and Van Rensburg (2015), Brand et al (2017) and Morrison et al (2017), have been incorporated into the review.

Those researching particular aspects of parental separation or divorce contributing to understandings of children's experience of: care in post-divorce families (Marschall, 2014); parental conflict (Roth et al, 2014; Francia and Millear, 2015); home after parental separation (Fehlberg et al, 2018); parenting coordination (Quigley and Cyr, 2018); courts' decision-making (Cashmore and Parkinson, 2008; Birnbaum et al, 2011; Birnbaum et al, 2012b) and young adults who had moved out of home at the time when their parents communicated the divorce to them (Abetz and Wang, 2017) were excluded.

The following 17 studies met the criteria and are included the review: Dunn and Deater-Deckard, 2001; Butler et al, 2002; Wade and Smart, 2002; Flowerdew and Neale, 2003; Moxnes, 2003; Hogan et al, 2003; Smith et al, 2003; Smart, 2006; Bagshaw, 2007; Campbell, 2008; Halpenny et al, 2008; Menning, 2008; Maes et al, 2011; Fortin et al, 2012; Du Plooy and Van Rensburg, 2015; Brand et al, 2017; Morrison et al, 2017. The studies were undertaken in Australia, Belgium, England, Ireland, New Zealand, Norway, South Africa, UK, USA and Wales.

Reference was made to two reviews of international qualitative literature of children's experience of parental separation; the first explored children's feelings about the separation and how their voices were heard (Birnbaum and Saini, 2012a) and the second the everyday impact of young people's experience in the intersection of home and school (Beausang et al, 2012).

The focus of each study, age of participants, size of sample and research location, are identified below:

- Dunn and Deater-Deckard (2001): study of English children's views about post-separation family changes and the support they received from family members, friends and formal support services during family transitions (aged 5 to 16) (sample: 456);
- Butler et al (2002; 2003): study of English and Welsh children's views, feelings and understanding of divorce and its impact parental divorce on their lives (aged 7 to 15) (sample: 104);
- Wade and Smart (2002): study of English children's views of parental separation and sources of support (aged 6–10) (sample: 242);
- Flowerdew and Neale (2003): study of English children who experienced 'multiple transitions' in their family life and the extent to which they were supported through them (aged 11–17) (sample: 60);

- Moxnes (2003): study of how Norwegian children who had experienced the most change in post-divorce arrangements coped with their parents' divorce (aged 8–18) (sample: 52);
- Hogan et al (2003): study of Irish children's experiences of family change following parental separation, their feelings about the separation, coping strategies and availability of support (aged 8–12) (sample: 30);
- Smith et al (2003): study of children's views of the decisions and processes involved following parental separation focusing on the initial separation, relationships with both parents and contact and residence arrangements. The study was conducted in New Zealand (aged 7–18) (sample: 107);
- Smart (2006): study of children who lived in a post-divorce family and the way they constructed a narrative account of their post-divorce family life to understand past experiences and develop an 'ethical disposition' in relation to family life (p 155) (aged 8–15) (sample: 60);
- Bagshaw (2007): study of Australian children's views, experiences and needs during transition following parental separation (aged 8–19) (sample: 19);
- Campbell (2008): study of Australian children's views about their participation in decision-making following parental separation (aged 7–17) (sample: 16);
- Halpenny et al (2008): study of Irish children's views on the support available following parental separation (aged 8–17) (sample: 60);
- Menning (2008): study of American adolescents' reports of the ways 'in which they manage negative aspects of their relationships with their parents' in post-separation households, their agency and strategies they employed (p 586) (aged 13–17) (sample: 50);
- Maes et al (2011): study of the meaning Belgian children constructed around their parents' decision to divorce and whether they felt that they 'mattered' in decisions about post-divorce living arrangements (aged 11–14) (sample: 22);
- Fortin et al (2012): study of English young adults' views of their childhood experience of parental separation and contact with their non-resident parent (aged 18–35) (sample: 398);
- Du Plooy and Van Rensburg (2015): retrospective study of how South African young adults coped with their parents' divorce during childhood years (aged 19–35) (sample: 15);
- Brand et al (2017): examined South African children's experiences and perceptions of parental divorce (aged 9–10 years) (sample: 5);

- Morrison et al (2017): retrospective study of how American young adults experienced their parents' divorce and aspects that have followed them into adulthood (aged 24–34) (sample: 9).

Seven themes emerged from a review of these studies, they are used as headings to report the findings in detail in the remainder of this chapter:

- parents' communication with children
- children's involvement in decision-making
- continuity in post-separation relationships
- parental support for children
- children's experience of parental conflict
- children's experience of post-separation family transitions
- looking back on childhood experiences of parental separation.

It should be noted when reporting the findings that the term 'parental separation' is used to refer to separation and divorce, the term 'divorce' is used when referred to specifically in the literature. This approach is used consistently throughout the book including when reporting the views of young adults taking part in this study.

What do children say about their experience of parental separation?

Parents' communication with children

Parents' communication with children prior to parental separation, throughout the separation process and post-separation changes was a dominant theme. Children wanted to be told what was happening, to have an explanation for events so that they could create 'meaning' and develop some understanding of the changes taking place. Dialogue with parents throughout the separation process assisted children in adjusting to the changed situation and was a consistent finding across the research studies.

Good communication started from the outset, children wanted to be told what was happening when their parents separated so that they did not feel 'left out' and were better able to deal with their feelings and anxieties about the future (Butler et al, 2002; Bagshaw, 2007). Most children were 'surprised by their parents' decision to separate' and many were not informed or warned about their parents' separation beforehand (Birnbaum and Saini, 2012a, 275).

One study found that two-thirds of the children in their study were told face-to-face about the separation by their parent(s) (Butler et al, 2002), another found only 5 per cent of children were given a full explanation and provided with opportunities to ask questions, of these children less than a fifth (17 per cent) were told by their mother and father together (Dunn and Deater-Deckard, 2001, 12). Where children were told by one parent, this was most likely to be their mother (Dunn and Deater-Deckard, 2001; Butler et al, 2002). When told by both parents, but separately, they received different accounts of what was happening, and why (Butler et al, 2002). In Butler et al's (2002) study one third of the children said no one told them, in Dunn and Deater-Deckard's (2001) study just less than a quarter (23 per cent) said this, but there were discrepancies in some accounts, with parents saying that they had told their child but the child saying this was not the case, age appeared to be a factor with younger children more likely to say they had not been told (Butler et al, 2002).

For children to construct 'meaning' about their parents' separation and come to an understanding of their situation it was important for children to know what was happening in their family (Maes et al, 2011). Where parents gave a clear, understandable reason for their divorce and children were told explicitly about it, they were able to discuss the situation and create 'an understandable story' (Maes et al 2011, 272). The iterative nature of this process was emphasised in some studies (Butler et al, 2003; Maes et al, 2011); children often felt 'the need to speak about it several times' and their understanding could be enhanced through dialogue with others such as a 'teacher, a stepparent, a grandparent, a psychologist or a friend', their understanding of the situation deepening over time (Maes et al, 2011, 272).

Some children were told about the separation only when new arrangements were put in place, when being taken to a new house or introduced to new partners (Butler et al, 2003) or when facing the 'sudden and unexplained absence of a parent' which led to considerable distress, confusion and sadness for children and was associated with unhappiness about post-separation arrangements (Hogan et al, 2003, 169). Children's lack of an 'understandable story' created through discussion with their parents was associated with difficulty in accepting their parents' separation and the changed family situation (Maes et al, 2011). This occurred where parental conflict was present and children 'sensed' something was wrong, but did not have an explanation, the distinction between 'sensing' and having an explanation was evident in their level of acceptance of the situation (Maes et al, 2011). Children consistently said that they wanted to know what was happening because it helped them 'to restore some kind of balance in their lives' but often they 'did not know how to ask for the information they felt that they needed' (Butler et al, 2002, 92; Brand et al, 2017).

Dialogue with parents combined with children's involvement in decision-making led to more positive feelings about living in two households (Dunn and Deater-Deckard, 2001) and enabled children to interpret issues as 'shared family problems' which had a positive effect on children experiencing a number of post-separation changes (Moxnes, 2003). Where children experienced reduced household income post-separation but had open, on-going and effective communication with their parents, they were more likely to express 'solidarity with their residential parent' and when it affected their lifestyle they were more likely to accommodate the changes (Moxnes, 2003, 135). This was not the case where children aware of parental arguments about financial arrangements became embroiled in wider family dynamics.

On-going communication between parents and children benefited those who experienced 'multiple transitions' (parent(s) re-partnering and the possible introduction of step- or half-siblings). Coping with change was easier where there were open lines of communication between biological parents and children (Flowerdew and Neale, 2003). These children felt that they had 'more resources with which to cope with change' and their accounts stood in sharp contrast to those where there were high levels of conflict between parents (Flowerdew and Neale, 2003, 155).

Children's involvement in decision-making

Three themes emerged in relation to children's involvement in decision-making about post-separation arrangements; first, their theoretical views regarding involvement; second, their own experiences of the extent to which their views had been taken into account; and third, the views of those who had been involved in decision-making as a result of court proceedings.

When asked their theoretical view of children's involvement in decision-making about post-separation arrangements, children's views being taken into account was a consistent theme (Butler et al, 2003; Bagshaw, 2007; Fortin et al, 2012). Having their views taken into account enabled them to feel 'appreciated and valued' and brought reassurance, this could also be seen in flexible arrangements that recognised their changing needs (Smith et al, 2003, 207). Children referred to having a voice, to 'fairness' and 'being respected' (Campbell, 2008, 246). This was a unanimous view among young adults, irrespective of respondents' own experiences of contact and whether contact had been a mainly positive experience or not (Fortin et al, 2012).

The second consistent theme was that children's views should be taken into account in parents' decision-making about post-separation arrangements (Butler et al, 2002; Moxnes, 2003; Smith et al, 2003; Campbell, 2008; Maes et al, 2011; Fortin et al, 2012). Views about how they might participate and the amount of involvement they wanted varied (Smith et al, 2003). While many thought that they should be consulted on issues that affected them as part of the decision-making process, age was seen as a factor by some (Campbell, 2008). It was noted how hard it was for children to respond when asked 'about their preferences' (Maes et al, 2011, 274; Smith et al, 2003) and while children thought that they should be asked their opinion about contact, often they did not want the burden of making the final decision, particularly in relation to residence (Butler et al, 2003).

Children said that having some influence and involvement in discussions about the separation and post-separation arrangements was very important (Butler et al, 2003; Fortin et al, 2012). They were more likely to be involved in decision-making about contact arrangements than residence (Butler et al, 2003; Fortin et al, 2012). Where their views were taken into account they reported higher levels of satisfaction in contact and residence arrangements (Butler et al, 2002) and more positive experiences of contact (Fortin et al, 2012).

One study, however, did challenge this view, finding that 'Children typically stated that they were happy with the arrangements their parents made and many strongly and unequivocally declared that they would not wish to be asked to contribute to making decisions of this kind' (Hogan et al, 2003, 168).

The particular cultural context as well as these children's involvement with support services may have influenced this view. Their involvement with support services would require parental consent, suggesting that their parent(s) acknowledged the benefits of their child being able to talk about the separation and access support outside the family.

Children emphasised the need to feel that they 'mattered' and were taken into account when living arrangements were discussed; it was less about the type of arrangements or 'having an active influence over the decisions' but about their living arrangements signalling to them 'that they matter to their parents' (Maes et al, 2011, 274). Such reassurance increased their sense of security (Brand et al, 2017).

'Having an opinion and being heard equated to feelings of being respected and valued in the child–adult relationship' (Campbell, 2008, 249).

The importance of children feeling that they 'mattered' was seen in other studies. Where parents involved their children in negotiations about moving house, about a step-parent moving or about contact arrangements, issues were seen by the child as a 'shared family problem' (Moxnes, 2003). Where children had information, felt able to discuss and express their views about whether there should be more or less contact with non-residential parents, or where contact was reduced, they saw the situation as being a 'shared family issue' with no one to blame (Moxnes, 2003, 139). These experiences were strong indicators of a positive adjustment for the child and were an important factor in the successful acquisition of residential step-parents.

While children were more likely to be involved in decision-making about contact arrangements than residence, overall there was a common failure of parents to consult their children about residence and/or contact arrangements (Butler et al, 2003; Smith et al, 2003; Fortin et al, 2012). This was despite 'even quite young children' feeling 'that they had something important to add' to these decisions (Butler et al, 2002, 96); or children 'being old enough to have clear views of their own, and being the principal players in these arrangements' (Fortin et al, 2012, 317). Instead there was simply an expectation they would comply with decisions, which most did until they reached adolescence (Fortin et al, 2012).

Young adults looking back on their experience were unanimous in their view that it was important for children to be consulted regarding 'critical decisions' and for their views to influence the arrangements made (Fortin et al, 2012). The study contained a few examples where children had made decisions about contact and residence, which as young adults they now regretted, they 'felt that they had been allowed to reach these far-reaching decisions at too young an age' and so were 'fully aware of the crucial distinction between consulting children and allowing them to make decisions' (Fortin et al, 2012, 330).

One study referred to children's theoretical views on judicial decisions in relation to post-separation decision-making (Campbell, 2008) and three studies included the views of children who had been involved in decision-making as a result of court proceedings (Wade and Smart, 2002; Smith et al, 2003; Fortin et al, 2012).

In Campbell's study (2008), children thought that if parents were struggling to decide on arrangements for the children, they should consult other people, such as members of the extended family, and most considered it inappropriate for decisions to be made outside the support of family and friends. They were also concerned about 'fairness' and the possibility of a judicial decision about residence being unfair to one parent. Another found while children enjoyed the meetings with Cafcass Officers, they lacked 'a clear understanding of the purpose of the meeting' and were 'unable to participate fully', leading Wade and Smart (2002) to conclude that

'They had no opportunity to voice their own agenda, or even to decide whether they wanted to make their wishes known' (p 38).

The need for this process to be child-focused and the importance of the adult developing a trusting and supportive relationship with the child so that they could participate and their voice could be heard was emphasised by Smith et al (2003), who concluded that children's views should 'be a regular and commonplace feature of family and legal decision-making' (p 211).

More detailed consideration was found in Fortin et al's (2012) study where 17 per cent of young adults said that their parents had been to court to arrange contact and/or residence arrangements. Usually, parents had been to court once or twice, although 3 per cent of young adults said that they had been 'repeatedly'; domestic violence and worries about the non-resident parent's care were often factors in these cases (Fortlin et al, 2012). Children whose parents had been to court once or twice were more likely to indicate that their views had been taken into account. The majority (82 per cent) felt that the court had 'made the right decision', only three felt that the decision was wrong, contact was delayed in each case (Fortin et al, 2012, 41). Interestingly, two respondents who said that their views were taken into account 'thought the court had taken *too* much notice of what they said' (Fortin et al, 2012, 41).

Continuity in post-separation relationships

Children emphasised the importance of maintaining good relationships with both parents and continuity in their living arrangements. They referred to the positive impact of maintaining contact with their non-resident parent and continuing to attend the same school so that they could maintain their friendship groups.

Continuity in relationships

The most noticeable, immediate, change for children was belonging to two households with different rules, arrangements and expectations.

They referred to the inconvenience of moving between two homes (Smith et al, 2003) and the practical difficulties – lack of space, 'having to constantly pack and re-pack bags' and spending time with parents' new partners (Butler et al, 2002, 97). They referred to the 'highs' and 'lows' of contact, the 'positive anticipation' of contact followed by the feeling of sadness when it ended and missing one parent when spending time with the other as well as the loss of spontaneity this created (Butler et al, 2002, 97; Brand et al, 2017).

In the early stages post-separation arrangements were often negotiated in the context of parental conflict, shock and an 'atmosphere of emotional turmoil and distress' (Fortin et al, 2012, 326). Contact arrangements could be a source of anxiety for children and effective communication between parents and parent(s) and child at this stage, served to reassure them (Butler et al, 2002). However, sometimes parents were pre-occupied with their own distress and adjustment to new family life and children experienced 'diminished parenting' (Fortin et al, 2012, 326). Where contact involved managing their parents' feelings and children were drawn into their parents' 'unfinished business' – being used as 'messengers' or asked 'intrusive questions by one parent about the other' – they faced particular difficulty (Butler et al, 2002, 97).

There was considerable continuity in parent–child relationships pre- and post-separation; the pre-separation relationship with the non-resident parent was the strongest indicator of the quality of contact post-separation and most likely determinant of the quality of the post-separation relationship (Hogan et al, 2003; Fortin et al, 2012). One study found that where there were changes, relationships with non-resident parents sometimes improved. This could be related to parents' adjustment to their new life or to the young adult 'developing a more mature and compassionate frame of mind', having moved on from the upset and anger which they had previously felt (Fortin et al, 2012, 328). Looking back as young adults some referred to their changed perspective on their own parents as a result of becoming parents themselves (Fortin et al, 2012).

Good relationships with both parents

Ongoing relationships with their parents played a key role in children's adaptation, relationships with their non-resident parent were particularly significant; those who adapted well, described relationships which either did not change, or improved, as a result of parental separation (Moxnes, 2003; Hogan et al, 2003; Halpenny et al, 2008). It was important for children to feel that they 'mattered' to their parents and where they felt that the relationship with their parent (usually the non-resident parent) had diminished they were often distressed (Wade and Smart, 2002, 11). They valued affection, emotional support and their parents taking an interest and an 'active involvement in their lives in meaningful ways' (Smith et al, 2003, 205; Fortin et al, 2012). Where contact was 'an enjoyable, child-focused experience' in which the non-resident parent demonstrated 'genuine emotional investment in their lives', respondents expressed high levels of satisfaction with contact (Fortin et al, 2012, 322).

Most children maintained contact with their non-resident parent (usually their father) after separation. Fathers who had regular contact were able to demonstrate their commitment to the child, which was crucial to successful contact (Fortin et al, 2012; Hogan et al, 2003; Moxnes, 2003). Children were alert to their non-resident parent's emotional investment in their relationship, contact between children and their non-resident parent was seen as 'vitally important in principle, it being a way of reassuring children that they are still loved and important to both parents' (Fortin et al, 2012, 4). This finding was consistent even among those young adults who did not have contact themselves or whose experience had not been happy (Fortin et al, 2012).

Children described individualised patterns of contact which took into account their school hours, their social commitments and parents' work commitments (Butler et al, 2003). After initial negotiations, contact arrangements tended to become regular and predictable but children emphasised the need for flexibility in arrangements (Butler et al, 2003; Fortin et al, 2012). No particular frequency, level or type of contact was seen as the ideal (Fortin et al, 2012). Children were often concerned to maintain 'fairness' in contact arrangements and 'equal treatment of their parents' even if this meant compromising their own needs or not always being truthful about their own wishes (Butler et al, 2003; Hogan et al, 2003; Campbell, 2008). A real dilemma for many children was sharing their time between family and friends – a particular issue at Christmas and birthdays – and was a situation that often persisted into adulthood (Butler et al, 2003; Fortin et al, 2012). Particular difficulties were created where young adults felt unable to bring their parents together to celebrate special events such as graduations, weddings and christenings.

The need for flexible contact arrangements increased as children grew older; parents' ability to adjust to and accommodate their child's needs indicated a more positive experience for the child (Fortin et al, 2012). Contact usually diminished during teenage years as children spent increasing time with their peers, where parents showed understanding and willingness to adjust to their child's increasing maturity 'an affectionate and secure relationship' was maintained (Fortin et al, 2012, 318).

Loss of contact with non-resident parent

Most children found losing daily contact with one of their parents a great loss but how great a loss depended on the amount of contact they had with that parent before divorce (Moxnes, 2003). The loss was felt keenest by those who saw it as the loss of something they valued and needed (Wade and Smart, 2002). There was some evidence that children, particularly boys, regretted the limited contact which they had with their non-resident fathers (Butler et al, 2003). For some children little contact with their father did not represent a change in post-separation arrangements, because their father worked away or the relationship was so poor it was not diminished by their absence (Moxnes, 2003; Wade and Smart, 2002). Where children had parent(s) unwilling or unable to negotiate contact arrangements and where there was a lack of explanation about why, they rarely had contact with their father, it troubled children and became 'a personal problem – they wondered if they were no longer lovable since the absent parent treated them in this way' (Moxnes, 2003, 140).

Sometimes the loss of daily contact brought a sense of relief because their father's behaviour often made them feel ashamed or frightened or their behaviour was over-controlling (Moxnes, 2003; Butler et al, 2003; Bagshaw, 2007).

On reaching adolescence, many who felt coerced into contact refused to comply, this was often related to what they perceived as the non-resident parent's failure to address their own weaknesses, for example depression, alcoholism, drug abuse or violent behaviour (Fortin et al, 2012). Some children maintained contact but employed particular strategies for coping with issues created by their non-resident parent's behaviour, controlling the flow of information, such as refraining from telling parents about their lives or telling the bare minimum or controlling contact by reducing contact or even changing residence (Menning, 2008).

One study found that 40 per cent of young adults who lost contact with their non-resident parent made contact with them in adulthood, grandchildren often provided a new focus (Fortin et al, 2012). Whether their parent was 'able to take responsibility for their part in the relationship breakdown and prepared to make the effort necessary to re-build the relationship' were important factors in its renewal (Fortin et al, 2012, 329).

Continuity in living arrangements

Moving house led to discontinuity in living arrangements and significant differences were reported between children who continued to live in the same house and those who did not (Moxnes, 2003). The distance between the old and new home as well as the extent to which parents were willing and able to help their children maintain existing relationships were key factors in children's adjustment (Moxnes, 2003). Where children experienced continuity in parental and extended family relationships, this was often assisted by family living in the same locality, which facilitated ease of contact (Maes et al, 2011). Children thought it was very important that siblings lived together in post-separation arrangements (Birnbaum and Saini, 2012a).

Attending the same school

Children saw remaining in the same school as particularly important, they valued the opportunity to keep in contact with existing friends who were able to provide support (Butler et al, 2003). Where there was the possibility of moving house, children feared the possibility of leaving school and the loss of friends or being unable to see their friends regularly (Butler et al, 2002; Moxnes, 2003). Finding new friends in a new community was very difficult, particularly if children moved more than once (Moxnes, 2003).

Children who experienced most change were more likely to show signs of negative effects of divorce than those who experienced one of these changes. How much stress they felt depended on the number of changes and the level of support from their parents and wider family (Moxnes, 2003).

Parental support for children

Parental support incorporated practical, emotional and financial support and was closely associated with the quality of parental communication and parent–child relationships. The influence of parental support on children's post-separation adjustment, parent(s)' ability to provide support and other sources of support available to children as well as the opportunity to talk to others were significant.

Influence of parental support

Where parents remained on reasonable terms with one another, children felt able to seek support from both parents and found them a useful source of emotional support, information and advice (Butler et al, 2002; Hogan et al, 2003). Inter-parental cooperation ensured that children felt comfortable in their relationships with both parents, and were reassured about their parents' commitment to a high level of involvement in their lives, these were positive factors indicative of a more positive adjustment to the post-separation family situation (Hogan et al, 2003; Moxnes, 2003).

The resident parent (usually the mother) was seen as best placed to offer emotional support and comfort (Butler et al, 2002). Most children reported an improved relationship with their resident parent after separation (Moxnes, 2003; Butler et al, 2003; Hogan et al, 2003). Often they attributed this to their parents being happier and/or themselves growing up; they felt that they got to know them better and there was more mutual respect (Moxnes, 2003). In the long term, children's relationships with their resident parents were more stable than those with non-resident parents (Fortin et al, 2012). Resident parents played an important role in supporting their child's post-separation adjustment through encouraging contact with the non-resident parent (Fortin et al, 2012; Brand et al, 2017).

The picture in relation to support from non-residential parents was complex and often linked to the nature and extent of contact and quality of their relationship. Many children reported difficulty in talking to their fathers about their feelings regarding the separation and they were rarely seen as confidants (Dunn and Deater-Deckard, 2001; Butler et al, 2003).

Some children felt unable to seek support from their parents because they thought their parents did not understand what they were experiencing, or had 'moved on' (Butler et al, 2002). In some cases, children recognised their parents were preoccupied with the changes in their own lives and they did not want to risk upsetting them further by talking about the separation or telling them of their concerns (Wade and Smart, 2002; Butler et al, 2003; Halpenny et al, 2008).

Parent(s)' ability to provide support

Sometimes parents were reluctant to talk about the separation because they wanted to 'protect' children from 'any further distress' (Halpenny et al, 2008, 317). A parent's ability to provide support for their children was often linked to their own post-separation adjustment. In some cases, resident parents did not cope well with the divorce, and instead of providing support for them, children felt that 'they had to "mother" their own mother' (Moxnes, 2003, 142). Parents could be pre-occupied with adjusting to their new family life or coping with their own distress, which meant that children lacked their support and experienced 'diminished parenting' (Fortin et al, 2012). Parental adjustment could be affected by additional factors such as health problems, addiction, violence in the relationship and financial worries, which meant that those parents were not emotionally available to support their children (Hogan et al, 2003; Smart, 2006; Brand et al, 2017).

In some cases, this reflected a short-term adjustment, but where 'diminished parenting' persisted for a long time, it often had an impact on young adults' attitudes towards that parent. As young adults, they referred to these parents in critical terms, describing how their parents turned 'to them for support rather than the other way round and parents ceasing to fulfil their parenting role' (Fortin et al, 2012, 316).

Where adolescents experienced an unsatisfactory situation which persisted over time, they tended to assess the parent's trustworthiness, motivations, what they offered them and how much effort they appeared willing to put into the relationship; if they viewed 'the relationship as beyond salvage or repair' they tended to end it (Menning, 2008, 611).

Sometimes the 'unavailability' of a parent meant that children felt the need to take on responsibility for their siblings (Birnbaum and Saini, 2012a). In such cases children often resented the demands made by non-resident parents, particularly when this left the resident parent with additional burdens. A lack of parental support and lack of parental cooperation during and following separation had a negative impact on children's wellbeing and children often told of 'disintegrated, damaged or lost family relationships and of having a broken family' (Moxnes, 2003, 144).

Other sources of support

Children's preferred source of support during the process of separation was their parents. Where this was available, children were able to adjust to the changes more easily, however extended family members were often identified as sources of support. In some cases they supplemented parental support, and where parental support was unavailable they often became a main source of support. Some children found support outside the family, often from friends who became confidants, some also spoke to professionals.

Extended family members

Children often saw grandparents as key confidants and a valuable source of support, able to provide 'time, attention and reassurance during periods of uncertainty', their homes were seen 'as 'safe' or 'neutral' territory in which to take refuge from what was happening at home' (Butler et al, 2002, 94; Dunn and Deater-Deckard, 2001). Children recognised and appreciated grandparents' roles in providing practical support for their parent(s) (Butler et al, 2002). Closeness to maternal grandparents (both grandmothers and grandfathers) was seen as indicative of an easier adjustment to post-separation changes (Dunn and Deater-Deckard, 2001).

One study found that the majority of children maintained relationships with both sides of the extended family, enabling them to draw on informal support from a range of family members (Hogan et al, 2003). Two-thirds of these children had attended the Rainbows programme, a programme designed to support children suffering loss through bereavement or separation which is delivered by trained facilitators. They referred to how it had created a safe space in which they could talk about their experiences (Hogan et al, 2003). The benefits of attending the Rainbows programme were reported in a further Irish study (Halpenny et al, 2008). Their experience was at variance to those of children in other studies and it may be their participation in the programme contributed to parental understandings of their children's needs.

Siblings could be a useful source of support, but often they were seen as too young, too close to the problem or had a different coping style (Butler et al, 2002; 2003). They might give different accounts of the divorce and some appeared to distance themselves 'from the emotional turbulence' of parental separation more easily than others (Smart, 2006, 164). Many found talking to their siblings helpful (Butler et al, 2003) but the availability and value of support available to children from their siblings was seen to vary.

Outside the family

Friends were often key confidants, they were particularly significant where children found it difficult to access support from their parents and were useful in enabling children to develop their own coping strategies

(Butler et al, 2003; Campbell, 2008; Dunn and Deater-Deckard, 2001). When it came to telling people about their parents' divorce, most children turned to their 'best friend' as a confidant. They found it easier to talk with friends who had experienced parental divorce because they were more likely to understand their feelings (Butler et al, 2002). Girls were more likely than boys to talk to a friend about the separation, but it was important that the confidante could be trusted to keep personal information out of the public domain (Wade and Smart, 2002). Boys often found difficulty knowing how to talk to others about what was happening (Butler et al, 2003). Friends performed an important role in offering diversion and distraction through peer support and the opportunity to engage in different activities including listening to music, playing games and sport (Butler et al 2002; Wade and Smart, 2002).

Talking to others

Some children felt 'embarrassed' to talk about their parents' separation even when this occurred some time ago and were discerning in to whom they disclosed their parents' separation (Wade and Smart, 2002; Butler et al, 2003; Hogan et al, 2003). Some reported not telling anyone, most often because they feared becoming upset if they talked about it. Sometimes they were embarrassed or ashamed about what was happening and feared being teased or rejected by friends which meant that they did not talk about it at school (Butler et al, 2003).

Children had clear expectations of what they wanted to achieve by talking to others, sometimes this was practical advice, but sometimes it was just having someone to listen (Butler et al, 2003). They found that adults were not always 'sensitive to or respectful' of their assessment of 'what they needed and how they wanted to be treated' (Butler et al, 2003, 69). School is a familiar place and teachers have daily contact with children so would appear to be well placed to support children, nonetheless children's experiences were seen to vary (Wade and Smart, 2002). Some teachers were seen as having personal qualities that might encourage children to approach them, but most preferred to keep their home lives private; they were reluctant to talk to teachers because of their authority role and the fear that they would be identified as having a 'problem' by their classmates (Wade and Smart, 2002). A few children found individual teachers helpful, but others had reservations about the teachers' ability or knowledge of how best to help and 'were particularly concerned about being the focus of unnecessary (and unwelcome) fuss' (Butler et al, 2003, 177). Often trust was an issue (Bagshaw, 2007).

Non-teaching staff such as classroom assistants and learning mentors were often seen as more approachable (Wade and Smart, 2002).

Children thought that teachers should be aware of changes in the family circumstances, however, so that they could understand the cause of any deterioration in their work or behaviour (Butler et al, 2003). Teachers were viewed as useful sources of indirect support through providing interesting lessons and the opportunity to mix with friends and the opportunity for discussion in circle time or Personal, Social and Health Education (PSHE) lessons (Wade and Smart, 2002).

Children who spoke to counsellors emphasised the importance of being 'in charge of whether or not information was passed on'; with discussions kept private unless they agreed to 'something being said to their parents' (Wade and Smart, 2002, 39). There were reports of children having positive experiences of using ChildLine, using this service meant that children remained in control of what information they provided and how it was used (Butler et al, 2002).

In their study Halpenny et al (2008) found that 67 per cent of children received support from a formal service, most often counselling or peer group support, most identified these as the most important source of support. Children described the positive effect of talking in a 'secure environment' which enabled them to gain a greater understanding of what was happening in their family, share their experiences with peers who were experiencing similar changes and develop trusting relationships with counsellors, knowing that their discussions were in confidence (Halpenny et al, 2008, 317). However, this was not always the case and some, particularly older children, referred to the fear of 'not wishing to feel different' and concerns about family privacy (Halpenny et al, 2008, 318).

Children's experience of parental conflict

The negative impact of parental conflict was a consistent theme, its presence posed a risk to children's social and emotional wellbeing and presented some of the greatest challenges to children's ability 'to cope with change' (Flowerdew and Neale, 2003, 155; Bagshaw, 2007; Beausang et al, 2012; Brand et al, 2017). Children from 'high conflict families', experienced 'greater stress and anxiety, greater fears and a narrow view of their world and future' (Birnbaum and Saini, 2012a, 276). Where parents were unable or unwilling to set aside their differences and cooperate for their child's benefit, children were seen to experience the most difficulty in adjusting to parental separation.

The incidence of parental conflict varied across the studies. Moxnes (2003) researched the experiences of children who had undergone the most post-separation changes and found that one in three had parents who argued frequently or fought after separation; they identified parental conflict as 'a painful problem that made them sad or angry' (p 143). Smith et al (2003) found that conflict over contact arrangements affected about a fifth of children in their study and was a 'source of pain and unhappiness' (p 206). Whereas Fortin et al (2012) found that almost three in five (59 per cent) young adults experienced parental conflict as a child; some described it as 'some bad feeling', others 'much arguing', others (26 per cent) described being 'caught up in parental arguments' while 19 per cent reported violent arguments between their parents or that one parent had been afraid of being harmed by the other (p 55). Parental conflict was often linked to contact arrangements particularly when it was delayed or sporadic, young adults spoke 'vividly of the corrosive effect of parental conflict' (Fortin et al, 2012, 322).

Where conflict was restricted to the time parents lived in the same household, separation often led to improved relationships between children and their parents. Children reported feeling more comfortable in their own homes and viewed the new family arrangements as preferable to those that existed previously (Hogan et al, 2003).

Where parental conflict persisted beyond separation, it often characterised a 'parent's relationship or parental style before, during and after divorce' (Moxnes, 2003, 143). Children referred to the divided loyalties and significant emotional burden it created, its negative impact on children's long-term adjustment and relationships with parent(s) was evident (Dunn and Deater-Deckard, 2001; Butler et al, 2002; Moxnes, 2003; Smart, 2006; Bagshaw, 2007). Contact handovers presented particular difficulties with parents 'bad-mouthing' each other, which caused children to feel 'torn by their parents' ongoing conflict' (Smith et al, 2003, 206). Sometimes children were used to act as 'messenger' between their parents or were asked 'intrusive questions by one parent about the other', in this way contact became an opportunity for parents to continue their 'unfinished business' (Butler et al, 2002, 97). Children referred to feeling 'caught in the middle' of the conflict (Bagshaw, 2007) often feeling that 'they were not allowed to love the "guilty" parent, while others felt guilty themselves when they "hated" that parent' (Moxnes, 2003, 143). They often became resentful of the demands made by the non-resident parent (Butler et al, 2003).

Children wanted parental conflict to end and for their parents to be civil and respectful towards each other (Hogan et al, 2003). They were very sensitive to criticism of one parent by the other (Dunn and

Deater-Deckard, 2001), and found parents making 'disparaging remarks about each other' upsetting (Hogan et al, 2003, 174). They frequently expressed the wish that they 'could at least "speak as friends" when it came to matters concerning' them (Butler et al, 2002, 98).

Where there was a high level of on-going conflict and parents were unable or unwilling to set aside their arguments and cooperate for the sake of their child, children had most difficulty in adjusting to post-separation changes (Moxnes, 2003; Bagshaw, 2007). In such cases, children felt unable to voice any concerns about post-divorce arrangements for fear that this would fuel the 'hostility' or 'aggravate matters' 'their choices were either to side with one parent...or to become very isolated with the feeling that they were quite without adult support as they navigated their own problems with growing up or the additional ones caused by their parents' behaviour' (Smart, 2006, 166)

Children's experience of post-separation family transitions

Children saw the process of acquiring step-parents as important, their experience differed significantly according to whether they were resident or non-resident step-parents (or partners). The number of changes, as well as the pace and timing of post-separation family transitions, had an impact on children's experiences.

Children described the introduction of a step-parent as a stressful event in their lives. The process through which they were acquired was very significant, in the case of residential step-parents this was usually a gradual process which allowed the child to become comfortable with the step relationship over time (Butler et al, 2003; Hogan et al, 2003). There was often a long process of negotiation during which a child had time to get to know the step-parent and contribute to discussions about them moving into the shared home (Moxnes, 2003). Where the pace of change was 'measured and comfortable' children experienced an easier adjustment. This was a result of being given the 'psychological travelling time' needed to accept and come to terms with this major life change (Flowerdew and Neale 2003, 153; Butler et al, 2003; Hogan et al, 2003; Moxnes, 2003). The number of re-partnerings parents had, as well as the timing of re-partnering was important, it was advantageous to children 'if only *one* parent re-partnered more than once', and 'if only one parent is re-partnering at *any one time*' (Flowerdew and Neale, 2003, 152).

In most cases resident step-parents were stepfathers, and were spoken of in positive terms. Where stepfathers contributed to household tasks, did not interfere too much in children's lives and contributed financially to the household, they were seen to make a positive contribution to the family (Moxnes, 2003; Flowerdew and Neale, 2003). Many children emphasised the economic benefits of stepfamily life, the new activities in which they became involved and the help step-parents provided in their day-to-day lives, in such situations stepfathers were viewed positively irrespective of the child's age at the time of transition (Flowerdew and Neale, 2003; Brand et al, 2017). The parent's happiness was also an important factor in children's acceptance of new partners (Flowerdew and Neale, 2003; Moxnes, 2003; Brand et al, 2017).

Where children expressed dissatisfaction or distanced themselves from their resident stepfather it often came from difficulties in moving house, living with new stepsiblings, 'negotiating new "ground rules", adjusting to new family routines and 'learning to "share"' parents and domestic spaces' (Flowerdew and Neale, 2003, 151; Moxnes, 2003).

Children experienced the introduction of non-residential step-parents very differently, with many meeting this person for the first time after they had moved to live with their parent; these introductions were rarely done skilfully (Moxnes, 2003; Butler et al, 2003). When a parent gave priority to their new partner/spouse and/or stepsiblings, children often felt resentment and anxious about their parent's commitment to them (Moxnes, 2003; Bagshaw, 2007). When this occurred in adolescence, young people often understood it as their parent's lack of emotional investment in their relationship which sometimes led to contact ending because they were so angry with their non-resident parent (Fortin et al, 2012).

When both parents re-partnered more than once or re-partnered at the same time, children found it difficult to accept and come to terms with post-separation changes because they did not have sufficient 'psychological travelling time' (Flowerdew and Neale, 2003). In such situations, changes were 'condensed into too brief a time frame in which there had been little or no time for recovery', adjustment was strongly influenced by the quality of the relationships as well as the extent to which children were able to exert some control over the changes they experienced (Flowerdew and Neale, 2003, 153). If unsupported and unable to exert influence children faced 'multiple challenges' (Flowerdew and Neale, 2003).

The timing of family transitions also influenced children's adjustment; where children's accounts showed family transitions occurring at the same time as other events such as General Certificate of Secondary Education (GCSE) exams or financial difficulties, their adjustment tended to be more difficult (Flowerdew and Neale, 2003). Parental same-sex re-partnering could present particular challenges especially where this coincided with children's own emerging sexual identity (Flowerdew and Neale, 2003).

Over time these changes and transitions became 'everyday problems' for many young people and were often overshadowed by other issues in their lives, leading Flowerdew and Neale to argue for a 'de-centring of divorce' in order to provide 'a more nuanced understanding' of children's experiences 'at key times in their lives' (2003, 158). In their view this would lead to a greater understanding of how risk and resiliency factors work and the opportunity to provide support for children if necessary (Flowerdew and Neale, 2003).

Looking back on childhood experiences of parental separation

The time that had passed since separation varied across the studies. With the passage of time children adjusted to a new 'normality' with the ability to reflect on their experiences, they developed their own views of what had happened within their family, were aware of their role within it and 'the part they had played and, potentially, could play in actively affecting relationships and arrangements in the family' (Hogan et al, 2003, 177).

As they looked back, the majority of children across the studies felt that things had worked out for the best. Some saw the experience as having benefits, their parents were happier and they felt that they themselves had become more grown-up, a 'better person' or gained in self-confidence (Butler et al, 2002; Brand et al, 2017). Reflecting on their experience enabled children to develop accounts of their personal experiences and to create ethical dispositions about adult relationships and how parents should behave towards their children (Smart, 2006).

Young adults, able to look back over a much longer period, often had a different perspective and interpretation of their parents' separation and post-separation events to those held when they were a child (Fortin et al, 2012). Many, whose non-resident parents did not maintain contact with them, changed their interpretation of why, many changed from a positive interpretation to a negative interpretation, but almost the same number changed in the opposite direction, suggesting that 'They had not necessarily acquired any greater understanding of past events, merely a different one' (Fortin et al, 2012, 330).

Some changed their attitude towards their own decision-making, seeing the decision not to have contact as a response to holding their non-resident parent responsible for the separation. This was often a strong view held in adolescence, which sometimes persisted into adulthood, but the passage of time and maturity could bring a change of attitude. When this happened a 'more tolerant and sympathetic outlook' could be developed resulting in greater understanding and acceptance of the circumstances that led to the separation and recognition of their parents' incompatibility, which sometimes led to an improved relationship with their non-resident parent (Fortin et al, 2012, 330).

Their changed perspective was sometimes influenced by changes in their own lives. Becoming a parent often encouraged a new perspective and where their parent(s) were able to acknowledge their behaviour it was often possible for relationships to be 'renegotiated', particularly when grandparents were able to assist with childcare arrangements (Fortin et al, 2012).

Open communication with parents about the divorce helped children develop an understanding of what was happening, what to expect and achieve 'some level of "acceptance" of the divorce and the resulting changes' at that time (Morrison et al, 2017, 50). They benefited from having 'someone to talk to' during the experience, particularly someone who had similar experiences, whether this was family members or friends. This helped in guiding expectations and normalising feelings so that children did not 'feel alone, different or confused' (Morrison et al, 2017, 51).

Extended family, friends and romantic partners also served as a distraction, and on occasions children moved in with them on a temporary basis (Du Plooy and Van Rensburg, 2015). They explained how focusing on their education, hobbies, extracurricular activities at school, listening to music and physical exercise were effective distraction and avoidance strategies. Some found that their spiritual beliefs helped them cope with their parents' divorce, enabling them 'to find solace and comfort' (Du Plooy and Van Rensburg, 2015, 503). Many young adults felt that their 'persistence' through the changes helped them to cope with the event, and 'reappraisal' or 'reframing' of events enabled them to view the situation from a different perspective (Du Plooy and Van Rensburg, 2015, 495).

Children's experience of parental communication shaped how they perceived the divorce and their parents. Those experiencing parental conflict developed stronger negative views. This often had an impact on their confidence in decision making and interactions with others as adults, including romantic relationships (Morrison et al, 2017). 'Most adult children [came] to accept their parents' decision to divorce as being the best option given the state of their marriage.' The quality of communication and level of support which they received at the time were critical factors in their adjustment and had implications for future romantic relationships (Morrison et al, 2017, 57).

Difficulties in parent–child communication, numerous changes, parental conflict and parent(s)' difficulty in coping, were factors found to hinder children's coping and support findings in previous studies.

Summary

This body of research giving 'voice' to children's experience of parental separation provides insights into children's experiences and their thoughts and feelings about the changes that took place following their parents' separation. Key themes emerging from the studies allow areas for further enquiry to be identified and ensure that this study is grounded in what is already known about children's experience of parental separation.

While the studies sought to access children's 'voice', parents mediated and controlled children's participation. All the studies involving children required the consent of a parent before the child could be approached to see whether they were willing to participate and if so, provide their assent, in this way parent(s) act as gatekeepers to participation and are able to silence children's voices (Birnbaum et al, 2012a). Some parents gave reasons why their child should not participate in a study (Butler et al, 2003), there were also examples of children wanting to take part and being unable to because parental consent had not been given (Wade and Smart, 2002). The requirement to obtain parental consent acts as an effective way of silencing, suppressing or ignoring children's voices. It means that adults are not presented 'with provocative accounts that challenge many of the taken-for-granted assumptions about what children do or think' (James, 2007, 264) and in failing to acknowledge the lived experience of children adults can focus on what they 'need or want when their relationships flounder' (Butler et al, 2002, 99).

Young adults who experienced parental separation in childhood have a particular contribution to make to our understanding of children's experience; with the passage of time they have the opportunity to reflect on their childhood experience, to consider what happened, the changes that took place and re-evaluate events. Over time the shape and form of their post-separation family situation becomes clear, relationships settle and, aware of their family's dynamics, they develop strategies for living within the changed family situation. Their perspective offers particular insights and yet their voices are largely absent from the research on childhood experiences of parental separation. This study addresses this gap in the research knowledge, the way in which it does this is explained in Chapter Three (The research study), which outlines the aims of the study and explains how young people were involved in the research design and construction of the research tools.

THREE

The research study

This chapter describes the research study in four parts. The first part outlines the aims of the study and explains how young people were involved in the research design and co-creation of specific research tools to undertake the study, a process involving the creation of a bricolage. The research tools involved developing a video clip of a fictionalised case study known as a 'prompt simulation video' (PSV) and creating an online questionnaire. The PSV, uploaded alongside the questionnaire, acted as a prompt for respondents' reflections on their childhood experience of parental separation. The research tools are described in the first part of the chapter where consideration is given to the benefits as well as the challenges of working in this way.

The second part of the chapter describes the study sample and population characteristics. It provides information about the respondents who took part in the study, including their current age as well as their age at the time of separation, providing a guide to the amount of time that had passed since their parents separated.

The data analysis process is described in the third part of the chapter. The data was analysed according to young adults' views of their childhood experience of parental separation with a focus on their 'accommodation' of post-separation changes over time. Responses to a question which asked respondents how they felt about the changes now were categorised and positioned on Continuum 1 according to the level of 'satisfaction' (high, medium or low) they showed and on Continuum 2 according to the level of 'acceptance' (high, medium or low) expressed. Where the levels aligned across the continua, they were combined to indicate a respondent's level of 'accommodation' of parental separation and post-separation changes. This became the central category for analysis enabling aspects of their experience and factors influencing their level of accommodation to be identified, these were then used to create a new framework for understanding children's accommodation of parental separation and post-separation changes as described in Chapter Four.

The fourth part of the chapter reflects on the research methodology, outlining its strengths and weaknesses as well as the limitations of the study.

Aims of the study

The aim of the study was to give 'voice' to young adults' childhood experiences of parental separation, focusing on their everyday experiences; in doing so it sought to learn about their lived experience of parental separation, what it meant to them as children and how they feel about it as they look back now as young adults. Through this process childhood experiences could be understood in their own right and an understanding of how children 'accommodated' post-separation changes over time could be developed. Listening to young adults' voices enhances understanding of children's experiences of parental separation and post-separation changes and, if shared with others, including those working and living with children experiencing parental separation, can inform future approaches.

As a qualitative study which focused on lived experience, the study adopted a phenomenological approach in which the world was made visible and transformed by making sense of phenomena through the meanings people brought to them (Denzin and Lincoln, 2011). The phenomenon of parental separation was understood through the meaning young adults taking part in the study brought to it, it aimed to gain a clear understanding of their experience, what it felt like to be 'in their shoes' and to understand their point of view (Denscombe, 2017, 139).

Involving young people in the research design

The study adopted a participatory approach to research design and the involvement of young people was seen as essential in achieving the aims of the study. There were three main reasons for taking this approach; first, the need to maximise the chances of the study being of interest and engaging for young adults by creating a space where they felt comfortable talking about their experience; second, the opportunity to minimise the power dynamics inherent in the researcher–researched relationship; third, it reflected the personal value system of the researcher.

Identifying or creating a 'space', where young adults felt comfortable expressing personal views about their parents' separation, was fundamental to the study's success. As the researcher, I had research experience in this area (Kay, 2006) and particular knowledge from working in the Family Courts, but I was not necessarily best placed to identify an appropriate space or determine the most suitable research methods for giving 'voice' to their experience. I formed the view that a collaborative approach in which I worked *with* young people to design the study and select or construct appropriate research methods was required (Bagnoli and Clark, 2010). This meant that the study was not approached with a particular methodological approach or research method in mind, instead the research design and methodology was developed *with* young people.

Focus group

Composition

In the early stages of planning, I talked informally with a wide range of young people, a small number of whom showed on-going interest in the study. It seemed a natural process for them to form a focus group with the specific aim of informing the design of the study and selection of research methods. Thus over time the four individuals showing a sustained interest became the self-selecting focus group.

The group comprised four young people aged 16–18, three were female (aged 16, 17 and 18), one was male (aged 18), two had personal experience of parental separation. They knew me through my work with a youth group, as did their parents, in this way they could be seen as a homogeneous group, which may have allowed ideas to be exchanged more easily (Robson, 2011).

The main purpose of the focus group was to elicit their views about the design of the research study and to determine the methods most suitable for undertaking the study (Bagnoli and Clark, 2010). This was explained verbally to all group members and the parents of those aged 16 and 17; they were assured of their anonymity within the study and made aware that they could withdraw from the focus group at any time without explanation. Following this explanation each focus group member agreed to participate and the parents of those aged 16 and 17 gave consent to their child's involvement.

Discussions

A series of open-ended group discussion meetings were arranged to decide upon the methodological approach, it was agreed they would be about an hour in length and that I would take on the role of facilitator, helping the group to run effectively (Bagnoli and Clark, 2010; Robson, 2011). The number of meetings was not determined in advance, instead it was agreed they would continue until decisions had been reached.

At the first focus group meeting, the aim of the study and purpose of the focus group was reiterated after which members were encouraged to take ownership of the agenda and lead discussions.

They decided upon the following ground rules:

1. main discussion points would be recorded in written form and a summary agreed at the end of each meeting, when the topic for the next meeting would be decided;
2. all comments would remain anonymous;
3. the researcher would be present at meetings and take responsibility for noting the main points;
4. the researcher would take on the role of facilitator to help the group run effectively.

The focus of the meeting was the best way to access young adults' views about their experience of parental separation. They were unanimous in the view that the internet was the best place to conduct the study because it enabled young adults to communicate freely about their own lives in their own way, to say what they wanted, to whom they wanted. Discussing use of the internet more generally, they highlighted the YouTube website and explained how regular visits enabled them to 'keep up to date' with new information and current trends. Readers may feel that this could have been assumed, however such a view fails to take account of the rapid rate of recent technological change, with access to and the way in which mobile and computer devices are currently used, changing considerably in recent years (Markham and Stravrova, 2016; Cohen et al, 2018).

Having reached the decision that the internet provided the most appropriate space for young adults to talk about their personal experience of parental separation, attention turned to how it could be used. Future focus group discussions considered the suitability of different research methods, who should be the target audience and ways in which young adults could be encouraged to participate. There was extensive discussion and the development of ideas was not linear; however, the direction was eventually determined and the following decisions made.

Research methods

One group member suggested an online questionnaire was a possible method and others saw this as having a number of benefits, namely: respondents could complete the questionnaire at a time and place of their own choosing, meaning that it was convenient (Cohen et al, 2018); they could view the questionnaire and decide whether to answer a question or not, thereby avoiding being drawn into a line of questioning which they found uncomfortable; and their anonymity 'where not even the researcher knows who the person is' could be assured, encouraging more honest and greater authenticity in responses (Cohen et al, 2018, 148).

Consideration was given to how the study could be promoted in a way that engaged young adults' interest to encourage their participation. Discussions focused on the use of materials to act as a 'hook' to engage interest. Across the group visual images were seen as a powerful tool and the three older members referred to the recent use of case studies in their academic studies as an effective tool in their learning. Developing these ideas further, the group suggested an effective way forward would be to use a short video clip based on a case study of children's experience of parental separation to engage participant's interest which could be linked to the online questionnaire.

It was proposed that the case study should be a fictionalised account of children's experiences of parental separation based on my professional expertise which could be dramatised, filmed and linked to the online questionnaire. The site for the study was the source of much discussion, how to make it accessible to the target audience while ensuring participants' anonymity was a challenge. The YouTube site was proposed and given serious consideration.

Target audience

The group discussed an appropriate target audience and suggested that as the study sought the views of young adults, the undergraduate students whom I taught might be a suitable audience. They had prior knowledge of me and my research background, and therefore had trust in the researcher and could be assured of the authenticity of the research. These are significant advantages when undertaking research online. This approach had considerable merit but raised questions about how participants' anonymity could be assured. Discussion returned to the use of YouTube and it was proposed the URL link could be shared with students who could access this in their own time. This approach overcame any anxieties students might have about the possibility of their anonymity being compromised, if the university's virtual learning environment (VLE) were used.

Evaluation

There was no formal evaluation of the experience of being a focus group member but members' eagerness to contribute ideas, engage in dialogue and question each other's views suggested a sense of empowerment (Bagnoli and Clark, 2010; Robson, 2011). They appeared to enjoy the experience as evidenced by some members continued involvement in trialling the questionnaire, creating the research tools and initial data analysis (Robson, 2011).

The bricolage

My role as a bricoleur

Work with the focus group determined the research design, an individual approach was being taken to investigate young adults' views on parental separation and so specific research tools needed to be constructed to undertake the study. 'Bricolage' refers to a situation where current methods are unsuitable for addressing the research questions and different tools need to be invented; we were therefore involved in creating a bricolage (Denzin and Lincoln, 2011).

As the researcher I took on the role of 'bricoleur' to construct the new research tools, but I was working to create tools which were outside my realm of experience and skill set and so needed to continue working with young people to create the bricolage. There were advantages to this approach, it provided a sense of creative freedom, encouraged more creative thinking about methods leading to a study 'better suited and more relevant to young people', allowing data to be produced which was 'closer to the everyday realities of young people's lives and times' (Bagnoli and Clark, 2010, 116). Co-construction of the research tools by the researcher and young people also subverted the power relationship between us, for I was dependent on their on-going involvement to undertake the study.

Nonetheless, working collaboratively to create the bricolage was complicated and unpredictable, there was the need for constant dialogue, on-going review and for decisions to be articulated clearly (Kinchloe et al, 2011). The involvement of another group of young people with a different skill set to take on the role of actors and film maker to construct the PSV was necessary which made planning difficult. However, it provided an unforeseen opportunity; working with young people to create the bricolage meant that the process of data analysis was not set in advance. During discussion it was evident that they viewed the data that would be collected through different lenses, suggesting different ways in which it could be analysed; their views were taken into account when determining the process of data analysis (Denzin and Lincoln, 2011).

The prompt simulation video (PSV)

Drawing on my professional experience I wrote a fictionalised case study which drew on themes emerging from the literature, in particular parental communication, children's influence in decision-making about post-separation arrangements, the quality of parental relationships and the impact of parental conflict. I wanted to show how children within a family can experience parental separation differently, therefore a fictionalised account of three siblings' different understandings, interpretations and experiences of their parents' separation and post-separation changes was written. The case study was shared with focus group members for their comments, they considered the scenario realistic. A copy can be found in Appendix One.

Dramatisation

The next stage in the creation of the PSV was the dramatisation of the case study. This involved an approach to the university's drama department with a request for undergraduate volunteers willing to assist and resulted in two female and one male volunteer. Following a meeting to explain the creation of the PSV and its use as a research tool, they agreed to develop a script and dramatise the piece. The actors were aware that the PSV would be uploaded onto the YouTube website, which meant that it would be available in a public domain and they could be recognised. They were given the opportunity to remain anonymous, but wanted their work acknowledged so their names were included at the end of the clip.

Three meetings took place between the actors and myself in which the script was developed and revised until we considered it a realistic portrayal of the case study scenario (a copy of can be found in Appendix Two). Rehearsals were arranged which the film maker observed; I attended the final rehearsal. At this stage it was agreed that the dramatisation was an authentic representation of the case study and arrangements were made for filming to take place.

Filming

The film maker, previously a focus group member and now a student studying at the university, maintained an interest in the study and was keen to film the dramatisation and produce the PSV. The dramatisation was performed and recorded twice to ensure that everyone was satisfied with the production and it had been recorded accurately. After editing, the film maker arranged a viewing to show the clip to the actors and myself, we were pleased with the finished product and decided that the PSV should be uploaded onto the YouTube website. The film maker was also given the opportunity to remain anonymous, but he wanted his work acknowledged, so his name was included in the credits at the end of the clip. The actors and film maker were each paid an honorarium of £50 for their work.

At the start of the study the PSV was posted on the YouTube website and linked to the online questionnaire; it ended with a request for viewers in the target audience (undergraduates aged 18–30) who experienced parental separation as a child to access the link and complete the online questionnaire.

Online questionnaire

Construction

In constructing the online questionnaire, its length and balance of open text and closed questions was considered carefully. Some multichoice questions with radio buttons or check boxes, some closed questions with open text boxes for further comment as well as open questions with text boxes were provided (Denscombe, 2014; 2017). Attention was given to the amount of space provided for responses to open questions as this could influence length of response. The questionnaire was organised to enable respondents to move on to the next question if they chose not to respond to a particular question, thereby avoiding 'forced responses' and allowing choice about the information disclosed (Denscombe, 2014; 2017; Cohen et al, 2018). The online questionnaire used the computer program 'Survey Monkey'. A copy of the questionnaire can be found in Appendix Three.

Content

The study sought to investigate children's lived experiences of parental separation, what it meant to them at the time and how they felt about it now, thereby giving 'voice' to their experience.

Young adults' views as they looked back on their childhood experience of parental separation were of particular interest, so the questionnaire asked about their first thoughts and feelings on learning of their parents' separation (Question 8), their thoughts and feelings about the changes at the time (Question 14) and how they felt about them now (Question 15). Open text boxes were provided for responses. Drawing on common themes from children's views of their experience of parental separation (see Chapter Two) the questionnaire asked about: parents' communication with them about the separation and post-separation arrangements; their involvement in decision-making about post-separation arrangements; continuity in post-separation relationships and living arrangements; and the availability of support during parental separation. Parental conflict was alluded to when asking how they learned about their parents' separation but no specific question was asked. The questions relating to each of these areas are identified in this part of the chapter.

To understand how parents talked about their separation and post-separation arrangements, respondents were asked when they were told about the separation and who told them (Question 7) as well as what immediately changed in their lives once they realised that their parents were going to separate (Question 11). A further question asking how other family members responded to the post-separation changes (Question 16) allowed respondents to refer to anything that they considered important in their experience and provided the opportunity for them to refer to their parent(s)' responses if they wanted. Respondents were asked their age at the time of separation (Question 5) because this could influence how much information they were given at the time of the separation and the extent of their involvement in decision-making about post-separation arrangements.

A specific question asked respondents whether their views were taken into account when post-separation changes took place and if so in what way (Question 12), an open text box was provided for their response. This provided insight into their involvement in decisions about post-separation arrangements. However, these responses needed to be read alongside the question which asked about their thoughts and feelings about the changes at the time (Question 14) because respondents may have felt their views were taken into account without being asked about their views.

To assess continuity in post-separation relationships and living arrangements respondents were asked who they mainly lived with after separation (Question 9) and whether there were changes in their living arrangements, school or the adults with whom they lived after separation (Question 10). This enabled any changes brought about by their parents' separation to be identified and the level of continuity in relationships and living arrangements assessed. To gain a more detailed understanding of post-separation arrangements, responses to this question needed to be read alongside responses to questions relating to the quality of parental communication and availability of parental support during parental separation.

Asking respondents about the support available to them at the time of their parents' separation involved three elements. First, respondents were asked, who was a main source of support during post-separation changes (Question 13). Using a series of radio buttons they were able to select responses from a number of people including family members and friends as well as no one, an open text box was provided in which they could identify other people. Second, they were asked to whom they felt able to talk about their parents' separation (Question 17). This question used the same format with a series of radio buttons provided to select their responses from a list, including family members, friends, youth worker, social worker, counsellor and no one, as well as an open text box in which they could identify other people. Third, respondents were asked whether they would have liked the opportunity to talk to someone outside the family about what was happening and, if so, who that person might have been (Question 18). To explore ways in which future children experiencing parental separation might be supported, respondents were asked what information would have been useful to them at the time (Question 19) and what advice they would have for a young person whose parents are separating (Question 20).

The literature review highlighted the impact of parental conflict at the time of parental separation on children's experiences. After detailed consideration the decision was made not to ask respondents directly whether parental conflict was part of their childhood experience of parental separation but instead to construct the questionnaire in such a way that responses to some questions acted as an indicator of the presence of parental conflict. This was done by making reference to the PSV, which referred to parental arguments and the possibility of domestic violence. After viewing the PSV respondents were asked what they thought about the film clip and were able to choose from a range of responses which included 'it showed some of how I felt when it happened to me' and 'it was how my brother and/or sister responded' (Question 3). They were also asked whether, when they watched the PSV, there were any similarities to their experience and if so in what ways (Question 6), open text responses were analysed to check for evidence of parental conflict. In addition, parental conflict could be identified in responses to the question which asked when they were told about the separation (Question 7) which allowed the option 'found out by overhearing parents arguing' to be selected.

The remaining questions asked respondents their age (Question 1), their gender (Question 2) and whether they thought the case study was realistic (Question 4). Given the target audience, the decision was taken not to ask respondents about their ethnic origin to preserve their anonymity, as asking respondents their age, gender and ethnic identity may have enabled individuals to be identified.

Focus group involvement

The final version of the questionnaire was shared with focus group members, this provided the opportunity to trial the questionnaire to ensure that the questions were understood in the way they were intended and gauge how long it would take to complete.

Their feedback indicated that they thought the questions were relevant, appropriate and could be easily understood. They saw the format as easy to follow and thought respondents would be able to navigate it with ease, answering those questions they wanted and avoiding those they did not.

Ethical Issues

The study referred to British Educational Research Association's Ethical Guidelines (2011) and the Association of Internet Researchers recommendations (2012) to inform the process of obtaining informed consent and issues of identity and anonymity on the internet.

The opportunity to verbalise their childhood experience of parental separation may be beneficial for young adults. It can be useful to look back and make sense of thoughts and feelings, and may be of therapeutic or emotional benefit (Wolgemuth et al, 2013). On the other hand, reflecting on their parents' separation may prove unsettling or upsetting in some cases; young adults might be reminded of emotionally distressing experiences that have become less painful over time or asked to comment on events which continue to create personal difficulties.

It was important to ensure appropriate safeguards were put in place to address this possibility, which was done by ensuring that potential participants had sufficient information to provide informed consent and by identifying sources of support available to them in the event that they became distressed when taking part in the study or afterwards.

Informed consent

The study was to be promoted in sessions I taught. This meant that I would be able to provide information about the study's aims, content of the PSV and online questionnaire as well as information about my professional background and research experience. This provided the opportunity to explain that the target audience was those aged 18–30 who had experienced parental separation in childhood and for potential participants to ask any questions. A powerpoint slide reinforcing this and providing the URL for the PSV was shown at the end of the session. Those interested in taking part were asked to read the online information sheets explaining the research study and providing information about myself as the researcher after the session (confirming information already provided in the session), before accessing the URL, watching the PSV and completing the questionnaire.

This information provided potential participants with sufficient detail to make an informed decision about whether to participate. They were expected to read the information sheets before completing the questionnaire. To be assured that they had done this, the first page of the questionnaire read as follows:

Having read about the aims of the research study:

- I understand the nature of the research study
- I agree to participate in the research study
- I understand in any information provided, I will not be referred to by name and any details allowing my identity to be revealed will not be included in the research
- I understand that I can withdraw my consent at any time and that should I do so I can withdraw any unprocessed data.

By completing the survey, I give my consent to participating in the above study.

Respondents were asked to confirm that they were aged 18 or over by clicking on a radio button, the questionnaire was configured so that if they failed to do this, they were unable to access the rest of the questionnaire. This process provided a formal record that the respondent had been informed about the nature of the research study and had agreed to participate; submitting their completed questionnaire confirmed their consent (AOIR, 2012; Cohen et al, 2018).

Sources of support

The study provided sufficient information about its nature for those thinking of taking part to consider the emotional impact it might have on them and decide accordingly. However, participants might choose to view the PSV and start to complete the questionnaire but become upset when answering the questions. To address this possibility, participants were made aware that they could exit the questionnaire at any point prior to clicking the radio button at the end which submitted their responses.

Appropriate support services were also identified, participants were reminded of university support services as well as services provided by Young Minds, Gingerbread, Samaritans and the Young People's Advisory Service. Weblinks to all of these services were placed next to the PSV so that respondents could access them if they became upset at any point when completing the questionnaire. Ethical approval for the research study was sought from the university in line with university procedures and the application was approved.

Identity and anonymity

The age profile of undergraduate students fitted with the target audience and they were as likely to experience parental separation as other young adults in the UK, but authenticity of respondent identity can be a complex issue when using online methods, with researchers often taking different positions regarding online and offline data (Heath et al, 2009; Orgad, 2009).

Promoting the study to undergraduate students whom I taught as part of my work at university meant that the target audience was a closed group of undergraduate students, nonetheless placing the PSV on YouTube with a link to the online questionnaire meant that it was in the public domain. It would have been possible to place the URL link on the university's virtual learning environment (VLE) site for each of the modules I taught, thereby restricting the study's availability to the target audience but student access and use of the VLE can be tracked by academic tutors. Therefore, the decision to place the PSV on YouTube was taken to ensure respondent's anonymity and overcome any tensions emanating from the dual role of tutor and researcher (BERA, 2011; AOIR, 2012).

There was a certain element of trust in this approach which relied upon respondent's self-reported age and gender, as would have been the case with offline questionnaires, but this was considered preferable to using the university's VLE. Strategies were put in place to address the issue of validity, these included checking the plausibility of the data, looking at themes emerging from responses to identify recurrent themes and checking the data with other sources, in particular findings from the review (Denscombe, 2014; 2017). However, safeguards were needed to guard against focusing on recurrent themes to the detriment of individual respondent's voices, which would risk marginalising their experiences.

The study

The pilot study

The PSV was uploaded onto the YouTube website and linked to the online questionnaire prior to the launch of the pilot study. Information about the study, its aims and the researcher was provided in separate links attached to the PSV.

The pilot study took place in one week in the first semester of the academic year and was publicised to 74 undergraduate students taught that week. Students were informed about the study, its aims, the methodology used and advised that they could take part if they had experienced parental separation in their childhood. They were shown how to access the PSV and the link to the online questionnaire and given details of the URL so that they could access it after the session if they chose to particpate.

Many students accessed the PSV and viewed the video clip but only five respondents (1, 2, 3, 4, 5) completed the questionnaire fully, including Question 15 which was a central category for data analysis; three respondents were female (1, 2, 4), two were male (3, 5); their ages ranged from 18 to 27, two were aged 18 (1, 5), two were 19 (3, 4) and one was 27 (2). This information as well as the time passed since separation is combined with data from the main study in Figures 3.1, 3.2 and 3.3. A full list of respondents with their identifier number, age, age at the time of separation and gender can be found in Appendix Four.

Respondents who completed the questionnaire provided responses to almost all of the questions, suggesting that the structure of the questionnaire and the balance of questions was appropriate and analysis of the data provided reassurance that the questions had been understood in the way intended. Time spent devising the questions and trialling the questionnaire with the focus group proved fruitful because no changes appeared necessary. A concern was the low response rate, but it was hoped that making the main study available to a larger target group for a longer period – four weeks rather than one week – would encourage a higher level of participation in the main study.

The main study

The main study was launched one week after analysis of the pilot study data, it was promoted in taught sessions during a two-week period reaching 270 undergraduate students and remained open for a further two weeks, enabling students to access it during the Christmas break when they might have more time to participate. During this time 38 respondents completed the questionnaire, but those who did not answer Question 15 were removed from the data set, this left 29 respondents in the main study.

Twenty-four of the respondents were female (6, 7, 8, 9, 10, 11, 12, 15, 16, 17, 18, 19, 20, 21, 22, 23, 24, 25, 26, 27, 28, 30, 31, 33) and five were male (13, 14, 29, 32, 34). Their ages ranged from 18 to 30; five were aged 18 (10, 13, 21, 27, 30), nine were 19 (6, 9, 12, 17, 18, 19, 25, 26, 31), five were 20 (8, 11, 14, 23, 34), one was aged 21 (15), one was aged 22 (32), two were 23 (7, 28), two were 25 (16, 22), two were 27 (24, 29) and two were 30 (20, 33). The distribution of respondents' ages across the pilot study and main study can be found in Figure 3.1.

Across the study, respondents' ages ranged from 18 to 30 years. Most were in their teenage years; eleven were aged 19 years and seven were aged 18 years. Many were in their early 20s; five were aged 20, one aged 21, one aged 22 and two aged 23. Their ages reflected the usual age cohort found in undergraduate student populations. Seven were a little older, however, and could be considered mature students, two were aged 25, three aged 27 and two aged 30.

Respondents were most likely to have experienced parental separation before entering their teenage years; seven experienced it in their early years (0–4), five in middle childhood (5–8) and 15 in late childhood (9–12). Four, however, experienced parental separation in their early teens (13–16) and three as they moved into adulthood

Figure 3.1: Respondents' current age

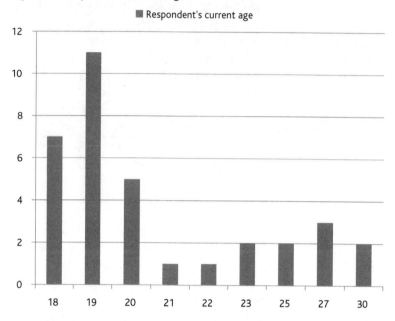

Note: Number = 34

(17–20). The distribution of ages at which respondents experienced their parents' separation can be seen in Figure 3.2.

From this data it was possible to establish the minimum time that had passed since their parents separated. This varied considerably, as can be seen in Figure 3.3. Most respondents experienced parental separation some time ago, 25 indicating their parents separated at least seven years ago. However, for four respondents it was a recent event occurring within the last three years and for five it had occurred within the last four to six years.

The process of data analysis

The aim of the study was to give 'voice' to young adults' childhood experience of parental separation and the questionnaire meant that respondents had the opportunity to describe their experience of parental separation and the thoughts and feelings it invoked. Questions prompted their recall of events and were complemented by the PSV which stimulated reflection. Determining the data analysis process involved attending to the study's audience, it was important that the findings were accessible to those who could influence the future lives of children, which meant that they needed to be represented in a way

Figure 3.2: Respondents' age at time of parental separation

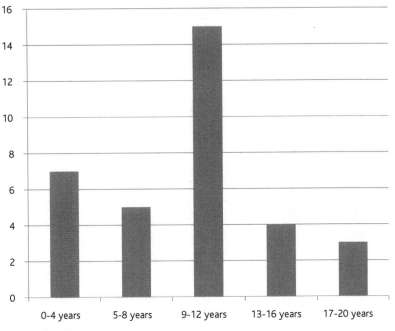

Note: Number = 34

that was meaningful to a range of audiences, including academics, practitioners, parents and young people. Consideration was given to the extent to which the findings should focus on individual narratives emerging from the data, or on their lived experience in which the essential features of these experiences were identified (Finlay, 2009).

Anticipating future use and dissemination of the study's findings, an analytical approach with a practical focus on lived experience was considered more suitable to meeting the aims of the study and the needs of prospective audiences. For these reasons it was decided that they would be reported through narrative commentary and in diagram form, enabling key factors and issues to be summarised and presented in an understandable and accessible way (Cohen et al, 2011).

Content analysis

The content analysis process was informed by Halling's three levels of analysis (2008). The first stage involved analysing the data collected from the online questionnaire through Survey Monkey, which was

Figure 3.3: Minimum time passed since respondents experienced parental separation

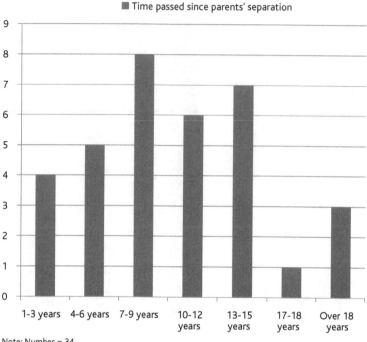

Note: Number = 34

displayed on an Excel spreadsheet, to gain a detailed knowledge and understanding of young adults' individual experiences through the stories they told. This involved taking detailed notes of individual respondent's accounts from open text and closed responses so that their lived experience could be viewed in its entirety.

The second stage involved three separate steps. The first involved listening to the 'voice' of the respondents by reading through each account carefully several times to take meaning from the account and ensure faithful interpretation of what was being read. This required an open attitude, what was known already about the phenomenon needed to be 'bracketed' and any 'prejudices, preconceptions and beliefs' suspended (Dowling and Cooney, 2012, 23; Denscombe, 2014; 2017). In this way the phenomenon, 'parental separation' could be seen through the eyes of those who had experienced it (Denscombe, 2014; 2017). However, their 'voices' needed to be represented, involving the researcher in an interpretive process, choosing what to present, how to present it and selecting phrases to illustrate points; detailed notes were therefore made of emergent themes (James, 2007; Clough and Nutbrown, 2012).

The second and third steps in this stage involved importing external frameworks to provide lenses through which the data could be interpreted and respondent's lived experiences understood (Finlay, 2009). The first lens was the external framework of themes emerging from a review of the literature (see Chapter Two), these were used to question aspects of experience, identify patterns of similarity and difference as well as clusters of experience. The second lens was the external framework of insights from my professional experience, which was used to test out interpretation of the data and understandings reached so far. These steps are considered in more detail in the section on 'Identifying experiences and factors influencing levels of accommodation' later in the chapter.

Respondent's accommodation of parental separation and post-separation changes

Categorising responses

Having read through respondent's accounts to understand their experience, responses to Question 15, which asked how they felt about the post-separation changes now, became the specific focus. These responses reflected the extent to which respondents had adjusted to post-separation changes or 'accommodated' the changes over time and they became the central category for data analysis.

The term 'accommodation' was used to indicate the extent to which respondents had adjusted to their parents' separation and the changes it brought over time. Used in a Piagetian sense it indicated 'old schemes' of understanding had incorporated new knowledge and understandings, and been 'adjusted to better fit with the demands of the environment' (Keenan and Evans, 2009, 158). Such knowledge might include more information about their parents' separation and circumstances at the time, the development of new relationships, understandings brought about by their adjustment over time or increasing maturity.

To gain deeper understanding of their 'accommodation', the term needed deconstructing. Knowing whether respondents were 'satisfied' with the post-separation changes, in terms of whether their 'wishes, expectations or needs' had been fulfilled was significant in understanding their experience (Oxford English Dictionary, 2012) but it was also important to understand the extent to which they 'accepted' their changed family situation, for it is possible to feel expectations or needs have been met without necessarily 'accepting' them. Therefore, it was necessary to understand the extent to which young adults viewed the process 'as adequate, valid, or suitable' (Oxford English Dictionary, 2012), in other words they had accepted these changes.

Consequently, the decision was taken to interpret responses to the question twice: first, according to the level of satisfaction respondents expressed, in terms of the extent to which their expectations and needs had been met in post-separation arrangements and second, according to the level of acceptance expressed, in terms of the extent to which they viewed post-separation changes as adequate or suitable.

Levels of satisfaction: Continuum 1

The following categories were constructed to reflect different levels of satisfaction expressed in responses:

- 'high' level of satisfaction indicated a positive improvement in their life, sometimes with occasional reservations;
- 'medium' level of satisfaction indicated neither a positive improvement nor a significant loss;
- 'low' level of satisfaction indicated a remaining sense of loss but greater understanding or a very significant loss in their lives.

Individual responses were categorised and positioned in one of these levels and a continuum reflecting the different levels of satisfaction constructed, this was referred to as Continuum 1.

Levels of acceptance: Continuum 2

Responses were then analysed according to the level of acceptance expressed, the following categories were constructed to reflect the different levels of acceptance expressed:

- 'high' level of acceptance indicated full acceptance of the post-separation changes, occasionally there was a little hesitancy;
- 'medium' level of acceptance indicated neither a negative nor a positive view – 'it is as it is';
- 'low' level of acceptance indicated a struggle to accept the post-separation changes.

Individual responses were categorised and positioned in one of these levels and a second continuum reflecting the different levels of acceptance constructed, this was referred to as Continuum 2.

To ensure consistency in categorising responses, an academic colleague and focus group members were approached with a request that they review the responses independently and categorise them according to the levels of satisfaction and acceptance outlined above. Two focus group members were able to assist and an academic colleague agreed to act as a critical friend in undertaking this process. In categorising responses, across the group there was an initial match of 85 per cent, five responses required further discussion before consensus was reached across the whole sample.

The next step involved looking at the level of satisfaction and level of acceptance expressed in each response. Where these aligned a respondent's level of accommodation of parental separation and post-separation changes could be established and assessed as high, medium or low. Most but not all responses aligned, but where responses were categorised at different levels across Continuum 1 (satisfaction) and Continuum 2 (acceptance), they were seen to lack continuity and a respondent's level of accommodation could not be established. Responses were colour coded according to the different levels for ease of reference. These levels became the central phenomena around which all other categories were identified and integrated (Cohen et al, 2011).

Identifying experiences and factors influencing levels of accommodation

Having established respondents' levels of accommodation where possible, attention turned to themes emerging from individual accounts to identify experiences and factors influencing their level of accommodation.

The process involved three steps: the first involved re-reading each account, listening carefully to the 'voice' of the young adult and what they had to say about the experience; the second involved importing external frameworks to provide lenses for viewing and interpreting their experience, the first framework comprised themes emerging from the research literature on children's experience of parental separation, the second framework was my previous professional experience.

The frameworks provided different lenses for understanding respondents' experiences. Undertaking thematic content analysis in this way, involved a 'dialectical dance', moving between 'abstraction' in which themes were drawn from the data and 'experience' in which research literature and my professional experience were used as lenses to interpret the data and extrapolate meaning from respondent's accounts (Finlay, 2009). Through these processes, certain themes and clusters of meaning emerged as universal aspects of children's experiences influencing their level of accommodation.

The third step involved probing these themes to highlight aspects of experience, build linkages, corroborate responses and draw conclusions about the ease with which young adults accommodated parental separation and post-separation changes over time (Jarrett and Odoms-Young, 2013). Associations and connections between ideas were identified allowing trends and patterns as well as differences to be noted. Where clusters of meaning occurred it was important to identify whether a common theme united several units of meaning (Cohen et al, 2011). Individual variations were noted and tested to see whether they were 'unique' to an individual or common to a group of respondents and could contribute to a greater understanding of children's experiences.

The final part of the chapter reflects on the research methodology, its strengths and weaknesses as well as the limitations of the study.

Reflections on research methodology

Working with young people to design the research and construct appropriate research tools, we created a bricolage which incorporated the PSV and online questionnaire. As a bricoleur, I drew on previous professional experience to write a fictionalised case study scenario, develop an online questionnaire and support young people in the creation of the PSV. The study adopted an individualistic approach, allowing circumstances to shape the methods employed and the new tools constructed to undertake the investigation, it involved each of us becoming 'a kind of professional do-it-yourself[er]' (Denzin and Lincoln, 2011, 4). Young people's involvement in the research design was invaluable, not only in ensuring the required skill set was available to create the bricolage, but also that the tools constructed would engage the interest of the target audience.

As a small-scale qualitative study, the study sought to give 'voice' to young adults' childhood experiences of parental separation, to learn about and understand how they experienced this life event at the time and how they saw it as they looked back, indicating their accommodation over time. Focusing on their experience it aimed to see things through their eyes, 'to understand what it feels like to be "in their shoes"' and to understand things from their point of view (Denscombe, 2017, 139). It did not seek to quantify experiences, to prove or disprove previous research findings, and consequently did not rely on a specific number of participants for the findings to be meaningful.

Its success in achieving these aims can be gauged by the number of completed questionnaires and quality of responses. The PSV was viewed extensively. Forty-five respondents went on to complete the online questionnaire, unfortunately only 34 provided responses to Question 15 which formed the central category for analysis of the data, meaning that the remainder were excluded from the data set. On reflection, further refinement such as positioning this question earlier in the questionnaire, highlighting its significance or including a progress bar indicating how far through the questionnaire the respondent was, may have encouraged a higher completion level (Cohen et al, 2018).

The online questionnaire enabled respondents to complete the questionnaire without limitation of time, in an environment of their choosing and to comment at length about their experiences. There was evidence that this flexibility encouraged some to describe issues they found difficulty talking about with others, such as one respondent who said that this was the first time she had spoken about her parents' separation which occurred 11 years ago. Respondents' confidence in completing an online questionnaire highlighted the value of online surveys in generating honest and authentic responses about sensitive issues (Farrow and Arnold, 2003; Orgad, 2005; Whitty and Joinson, 2009; Cohen et al, 2018).

The PSV scenario resonated with many respondents who made a personal connection with it, either because they held different views about the separation to their siblings, and/or because parental conflict was a feature of their parents' separation. The questionnaire provided the opportunity for them to tell their story. Whether mentioning parental conflict in the PSV encouraged respondents to talk about this aspect of their experience, prompting them to acknowledge events often kept hidden and unspoken about is unknown, but 14 respondents referred to parental conflict in their accounts. If it is the case that the PSV content encouraged young adults to talk about parental conflict, this could present a bias in the study and it may well be that using a different case study scenario emphasising another aspect of parental separation could lead to different findings, which is worth considering in any future study.

The study relied upon data collected from online questionnaires which assured respondent anonymity. Aware of extensive debate about reliance on online data and the trustworthiness of such data, checks and balances were put in place to examine the validity and plausibility of the data. Respondent's age and gender relied on self-reporting, the information provided supported data relating to the student cohort, with males under-represented, as they were in the cohort. Each completed questionnaire provided a set of unique responses, all responses were fluent in written English and indicated the respondent was knowledgeable about the experience of parental separation. Taking these factors into account I had confidence in respondents' identities and while there is no way of verifying what someone says about their thoughts and feelings, their accounts appeared truthful and authentic (Denscombe, 2014; 2017; Cohen et al, 2018).

The data was examined in relation to recurrent themes and the extent to which they could be identified in analysis of the data, this gave an indication that issues were shared among a wider group (Denscombe, 2014; 2017). At the same time, there was a need to guard against privileging recurrent themes to the detriment of individual voices, for it was important that the voices of young adults who had particular and diverse experiences were not marginalised. Special care was needed when representing the voices of respondents who reported a low level of accommodation or whose response lacked continuity, as they constituted small groups and tended to report specific experiences.

Limitations

To ensure that their identity was protected, respondents were not asked about ethnicity, this decision was reached because of the target group used, the sensitive nature of the research and size of the cohort, protection of individual respondent's identities was seen to outweigh the need for this information. However, this information would have been helpful when analysing the data and contextualising individual experiences and may well have allowed greater recognition of cultural factors influencing children's experiences.

Male respondents constituted a fifth of the sample, reflecting their representation in the target group; their limited number meant that the influence of gender could only be inferred from the research findings and a larger male representation may have strengthened some of the tentative conclusions reached.

Within the study no direct reference was made to same-sex relationships and this could not be inferred from any responses, this is not to say that when respondents referred to their parents' partners it can be assumed that they were referring to opposite sex couples. This is an area worthy of further investigation in future studies; further discussion could be encouraged in the way questions are framed and expressed.

The next chapter (Chapter Four, Constructing a new framework for understanding children's accommodation of parental separation) reports the level of satisfaction (Continuum 1) and level of acceptance (Continuum 2) of post-separation changes found in respondent's accounts and identifies their level of accommodation. It goes on to explain how themes and clusters of meaning emerging from their accounts were used to construct a new framework for understanding young adults' accommodation of childhood experiences of parental separation. It describes the framework and explains how it extends our understanding and awareness of how experiences have an impact on children's accommodation of parental separation and post-separation changes.

FOUR

Constructing a new framework for understanding children's accommodation of parental separation

The aim of the research study was to give 'voice' to young adults' childhood experiences of parental separation; to understand what they thought and how they felt about their experiences at the time, what they considered important then, and how they viewed their experiences now, as they looked back as young adults. Understanding how they felt about the changes experienced during and after separation provided the opportunity to assess their accommodation of these changes over time and identify aspects of childhood experience influencing their level of accommodation. Analysis of the data allowed respondents' accounts to be assessed according to whether they showed a high, medium or low level of accommodation (see Chapter Three). Common themes emerged within each level and were used to construct a new framework for understanding children's accommodation of parental separation and post-separation changes. This chapter describes the construction of the framework and explains how the framework can be used to deepen understanding of children's experiences.

The chapter starts with an account of individual responses and explains how they were categorised and positioned according to the level of satisfaction (Continuum 1) and level of acceptance (Continuum 2) shown. Where the levels aligned, a respondent's level of accommodation could be determined according to whether they showed a high, medium or low level of accommodation, this is identified alongside the respondent ID number in this chapter. In some cases, responses showed a 'lack of continuity' across Continuum 1 and Continuum 2; these are identified in the chapter.

Once categorised according to their level of accommodation, further analysis encouraged a deeper, more meaningful understanding of individual experiences and the influence these exerted on their accommodation. By interrogating these particular aspects of their experience, a picture began to emerge of how certain childhood experiences influenced responses to post-separation changes and respondents' level of accommodation over time.

The nature of family relationships means that children's experiences are unique, the responses given were diverse and sometimes complicated. Nonetheless a range of factors and experiences influencing young adults' accommodation of childhood experiences of parental separation and post-separation changes could be identified. These were used to develop a new framework for understanding children's accommodation of parental separation and post-separation changes as explained in the second part of this chapter. Each theme within the framework is examined in detail in a specific chapter focusing on Reactions (Chapter Six), Support (Chapter Seven), Communication (Chapter Eight) and Conflict (Chapter Nine).

Accommodation of parental separation

The process of categorising responses to question 15 according to the level of satisfaction (Continuum 1) and level of acceptance (Continuum 2) expressed was explained in Chapter Three. The task was undertaken by myself, two focus group members as well as an academic colleague who acted as a critical friend. On completion we met as a group to discuss the categorisation, there was considerable agreement but further discussion was needed in relation to five responses in particular the responses of Respondents 22 and 29, each of whom focused predominantly on their adult lives. Discussion took place about whether comments elsewhere in their accounts could be used to determine their levels of satisfaction and acceptance. It was agreed that they could, because this provided a more complete and accurate picture of their experience, so long as this approach was applied consistently across the study.

The first part of the chapter records each respondent's response and shows how they were categorised according to their level of satisfaction (Continuum 1) and level of acceptance (Continuum 2). Responses are reported in either section alongside their respondent ID number and age at the time of separation, these are recorded at the end of the quote. The levels of satisfaction (Continuum 1) and levels of acceptance (Continuum 2) are reiterated here for ease of reference.

Level of satisfaction: Continuum 1

'Satisfaction' was interpreted according to whether respondents felt that their expectations or needs had been met and responses categorised according to the following levels:

- 'high' level of satisfaction indicated a positive improvement in their life, sometimes with occasional reservations;
- 'medium' level of satisfaction indicated neither a positive improvement nor a significant loss;
- 'low' level of satisfaction indicated a remaining sense of loss but greater understanding or a very significant loss in their lives.

High

Twenty respondents (3, 4, 6, 7, 8, 9, 10, 11, 14, 15, 18, 19, 21, 23, 25, 26, 27, 29, 30, 31) saw their parents' separation as a positive improvement in their life and were assessed as having a high level of satisfaction. Three common themes emerged from their accounts: first, how relationships between their parents were better after they separated (6, 8, 10, 18, 21, 26); second, how they had a greater understanding of the situation now they were older (4, 15, 23, 25) and third, knowing that their parents separating was best from the outset (9, 19).

Many experienced improved communication between their parents after separation, which had a beneficial effect on the parents' relationships as well as their relationships with their child, as noted in the following comments:

> 'Mum and Dad get on well now and it is much better.' (Respondent 6; aged 0–4)

> 'I feel great now, both parents are very friendly to one another and talk a lot.' (Respondent 18; aged 0–4)

> 'Both my mum and dad are happy now and they are in good relationships and I get on with them both.' (Respondent 10; aged 9–12)

> 'We get on fine now and they are both much happier with their lives and are able to speak to each other.' (Respondent 21; aged 9–12)

Sometimes it even brought about reconciliation as in the case of Respondents 8 and 26:

> 'My family gets on quite well now and my mum and dad have got back together.' (Respondent 8; aged 9–12)

> 'My parents became friends again and then got back together so things are good again now.' (Respondent 26; aged 9–12)

Often respondents said that they had a greater understanding of the situation now that they were older:

> 'Now that I am older I see it differently, my family are close, especially me and my mum. I am glad that my parents have separated because we like each other more and respect each other.' (Respondent 25; aged 5–8)

> 'Now I'm older I understand it more and think it was better that they split up. I understand why my mum made the decision she did. It was the right decision.' (Respondent 15; aged 5–8)

Some knew that their parents' separation was for the best from the outset:

> 'I knew Mum and Dad couldn't live together even though I wanted them to. It was obvious it was better for them to divorce. So even though it was really hard I knew everything would be better when they didn't live together and it would be OK in the end. Mum married someone else and that is fine as well.' (Respondent 19; aged 13–16)

Occasionally the absence of a parent improved a child's life, such as in the case of Respondent 29:

> 'My dad was a horrible man and it was great for us all to be rid of him to be honest. My marriages have not been happy but I am really going to try to make this one work for the sake of the kids.' (Respondent 29; aged 13–16)

Respondent 7 also described how her life improved after her mother's partner left, saying:

> 'I think it made me stronger.' (Respondent 7; aged 0–4)

Nonetheless, sometimes respondents expressed reservation about their post-separation family situation; feeling 'torn' was a feature of some accounts:

> 'Most of the time things are OK, but I feel torn a bit sometimes.' (Respondent 3; aged 9–12)

> 'It's all good now, still feel torn from time to time.' (Respondent 14; aged 9–12)

Sometimes the desire for direct contact with their non-resident parent was evident:

> 'Most of the time OK but I wish I could see Mum sometimes. Nan has been like a mum to me. I don't remember living with Mum and Dad, it was so long ago.' (Respondent 30; aged 0–4)

Medium

Nine respondents (5, 13, 16, 22, 24, 28, 32, 33, 34) viewed their parents' separation and the changes it brought as neither a positive improvement, nor a significant loss, and were categorised as showing a medium level of satisfaction.

The notion of distance, either emotional distance, or in terms of time passed, was a common theme in some accounts, particularly among male respondents aged 9–12 at the time:

> 'Pretty much over it.' (Respondent 13; aged 9–12)

> 'I've moved on.' (Respondent 5; aged 9–12)

> 'I'm distanced from it.' (Respondent 32; aged 9–12)

One respondent (16) explained how she had a better understanding of the situation now that she was older and that it was the best thing for her parents at the time:

'Now I am older, I have a better understanding and realise why things happened. It was the best thing for them at the time.' (Respondent 16; aged 5–8)

Parental conflict featured in some accounts and one respondent felt that if action had been taken earlier, her life would have improved:

'If I had told someone in authority sooner what was happening, [then] we could all have got on with our lives and been happier sooner.' (Respondent 24; aged 17–20)

Some described how they adjusted to their family situation, but commented on the impact family relationships have had on their adult life:

'I am used to the way our family is but I find it almost impossible to be close to someone and trust them. I have not had a long-term relationship, none lasting more than a few months because I cannot seem to trust people. I am not gay but I find it hard to be close to men. I don't know if this will ever change and if it is because of my childhood experiences.' (Respondent 28; aged 9–12)

Respondent 22 referred to her current role as a wife and mother, this made her response difficult to categorise, but taking account of comments elsewhere, the decision was made to categorise her response as showing a medium level of satisfaction:

'Now I look back and think that my experiences as a child have made me the person I am today. I am determined to be a good role model, wife and mother. I make sure I listen to my children and prioritise their needs so that they do not have the same experiences as me.' (Respondent 22; aged 0–4)

Low

Some respondents continued to experience difficulty adjusting to their parents' separation and post-separation changes, their responses tended to have a high level of emotional content, making them difficult to read. Their accounts indicated a sense of loss in their lives and therefore were categorised as showing a low level of satisfaction. There were five respondents (1, 2, 12, 17, 20) in this category.

In these cases, parental separation was often complicated by other factors, such as experiencing parental separation for a second time as in the case of Respondent 2, who explained how following her parents' separation she moved to live with her grandparents who then went on to separate:

> 'I still miss my granddad but I understand why they separated because Nana and he were not happy together.' (Respondent 2; aged 9–12)

Respondent 20's parents separated as a result of her father's imprisonment, she described the impact this had on her life when it became known in the community:

> 'When it came out we had to move house and I moved school. I never went to see Dad but he sent letters. I still have them but I don't want to see him. He was not there when I was growing up and so I don't want to see him now and given what he did I don't want him near my child either.' (Respondent 20; aged 0–4)

Sometimes there was evidence of a high level of parental conflict:

> 'It's really hard when your mum and dad hate each other. I suppose it's best if they split up, but I still get upset when I think about it. That hasn't got any easier because they still argue – in fact at the moment it's probably worse, I don't know why.' (Respondent 1; aged 9–12)

> 'At the time you have to get on with it, it can be worse now thinking back. But even then I knew that it was not fair that they made us feel like we did. Dad never hid that he did not like us seeing Mum and we all knew Mum hated Dad so it was hard going between the two.' (Respondent 17; aged 9–12)

One respondent (12) experienced her parents' separation very recently. It was an event which coincided with her move to university. She simply described feeling 'very sad' as a result of all the changes.

Level of acceptance: Continuum 2

Acceptance was interpreted according to whether respondents saw those post-separation arrangements that were put into place as adequate or suitable. Responses were categorised according to the following levels:

- 'high' level of acceptance indicated full acceptance of the post-separation changes, occasionally there was a little hesitancy;
- 'medium' level of acceptance indicated neither a negative nor a positive view – 'it is as it is';
- 'low' level of acceptance indicated a struggle to accept the post-separation changes.

High

Responses were categorised as showing full acceptance of post-separation changes when they indicated respondents had adjusted to the changes and embraced them over time. Sometimes respondents had adjusted to the changes, but expressed some hesitancy from time to time. Where this occurred their response was checked alongside the rest of their account for consistency and where this was found they were assessed as having a high level of acceptance because taken as a whole, this is what their account showed.

Twenty-three respondents (3, 4, 6, 7, 8, 9, 10, 11, 13, 14, 15, 18, 19, 21, 23, 24, 25, 26, 27, 29, 30, 31, 34) were placed in this category; with the exception of 29 this included all the respondents who showed a high level of satisfaction as well as three (13, 24, 34) who showed a medium level of satisfaction.

As a result of his parents' separation, Respondent 13 lost contact with his father for two years when he was 10 years old, it took time for him to reach a high level of acceptance of post-separation changes which was probably achieved on renewal of contact. Respondent 24's high level of acceptance reflected the relief she felt when her parents separated and parental conflict ended as a result of her father leaving the family home. In contrast, Respondent 34 experienced his parents' separation as he started university, he accepted the changes it brought, but expressed some hesitancy, as seen in his comment about whom he would see at Christmas. His response highlights the time that it can take to adjust to post-separation changes:

'Mum and Dad separated last year and so I have learned to accept they live separate lives now. This will be the second Christmas without them together. I don't think it will be as difficult as the first Christmas and I will be spending it with my girlfriend and her parents.' (Respondent 34; aged 17–20)

Some respondents reached a high level of acceptance as they grew older and gained a greater awareness and increased understanding of the separation and the changes it brought:

'Now I understand it was for the best and can see why Mum hadn't any choice.' (Respondent 4; aged 5–8)

'I can see now that we were all better for the split in the long run, my mum, dad, sister and me. In fact it might have been better even earlier. Although it is good that they met and had us in the first place.' (Respondent 23; aged 5–8)

'Things are much better now.' (Respondent 11; aged 9–12)

Although one respondent (9) always knew that her parents' separation was for the best:

'I know it was for the best; I knew that the whole way through. I think people expected me to be hurt, upset, angry, go off the rails, but I never went through any of that because I knew that life might have been a whole lot worse had my parents stayed together. Of course, it would have been nice if they did, every child wants their parents to get along, but mine never got on well and still do not today. I still think Mum remarried too soon though, but I don't resent her for that.' (Respondent 9; aged 13–16)

It was not unusual for those who accepted the separation and changes it brought to comment on how things might have been:

'It would be great if all parents could stay together, but actually I am happy and content now.' (Respondent 31; aged 9–12)

'I'm used to it. Mum and I get on great and I wouldn't change it but sometimes I'm curious about what it would be like to have a dad in my life.' (Respondent 27; aged 0–4)

Medium

Responses showing neither a negative nor a positive view of post-separation changes, but rather that their post-family situation 'is as it is' were categorised as showing a medium level of acceptance of parental separation and post-separation changes. There were seven respondents (5, 16, 20, 22, 28, 32, 33) in this category, six (5, 16, 22, 28, 32, 33) of whom also showed a medium level of satisfaction. With the exception of Respondent 33, their views are described in the quotes recorded in the section on medium satisfaction above (see page 71). Respondent 33's views are recorded below.

Many respondents appeared 'distanced' in their relationships with their family of origin, often through a loss of contact. This could be seen in comments elsewhere in their accounts; two respondents (5, 32) lost contact with their fathers and Respondent 28 lost daily contact with her siblings as she lived with her mother and they lived with her father after separation. Respondent 20 lost contact with her father as a result of his imprisonment and made it clear that she did not want her daughter to see him. She accepted the arrangements to the extent that she made decisions about how she would manage any contact her father proposed with her and her child, and therefore was categorised as having a medium level of acceptance.

One respondent (33) thought that it would have been better if her parents had separated earlier, but she realised that they had stayed together for her and her brother.

'It was a shame it took so long for them to finally separate and divorce but I know they wanted to stay together for the sake of me and my brother. I feel like it's one of those things and everyone reacts in their own way. I was very lonely at the time but don't think I realised it.' (Respondent 33; aged 13–16)

Respondent 22 focused on the impact her childhood experiences had on her role as a wife and mother (see quote above in the section on medium satisfaction (page 72)). Responses elsewhere in her account indicated that she still maintained some contact with her parents. It was not possible to categorise her response as a full acceptance of post-separation changes with occasional hesitation, so it was therefore categorised as a medium level of acceptance.

Low

Responses which indicated that respondents were struggling to accept post-separation changes were categorised as having a low level of acceptance. There were four respondents in this category (1, 2, 12, 17) all of whom also showed a low level of satisfaction. Their views are described in the quotes recorded in the section on low satisfaction above (see page 72).

Their accounts often referred to on-going difficulties in family relationships, including parental conflict which continued long after their separation (1, 17) or because parental separation was a recent event and post-separation arrangements were being determined (12).

Once categorised according to their level of satisfaction (Continuum 1) and level of acceptance (Continuum 2) respondents were positioned on each continuum as can be seen in Appendix Five.

Levels of accommodation

There was a high level of continuity across the level of satisfaction (Continuum 1) and level of acceptance (Continuum 2) meaning that levels could be combined to indicate a respondent's level of accommodation of parental separation in 30 cases. Of these 30 respondents, 20 showed a high level of accommodation; six showed a medium level of accommodation and four showed a low level of accommodation as can be seen in Table 4.1.

Table 4.1: Levels of accommodation: respondents who showed continuity across Continuum 1 and Continuum 2

Level of accommodation	Number of respondents	Respondent ID Number
High	20	3, 4, 6, 7, 8, 9, 10, 11, 14, 15, 18, 19, 21, 23, 25, 26, 27, 29, 30, 31
Medium	6	5, 16, 22, 28, 32, 33
Low	4	1, 2, 12, 17
Total	30	

Lack of continuity

In four cases (13, 20, 24, 34) responses were categorised differently across the continua as can be seen in Table 4.2. In these cases, responses lacked continuity across the continua and it was not possible to determine a respondent's level of accommodation of parental separation. Their comments are reported in Chapters Five to Ten, where they are identified as respondents whose responses 'lacked continuity' across the continua, but they are not taken into account in the construction of the framework or in discussion of the different levels of accommodation.

Further analysis of these accounts showed respondents had experienced parental separation in different ways and at different ages but most had lost contact with their non-resident parent as a result of parental separation. This was what two respondents (20, 24) wanted and was an informed decision by Respondent 24, aged 17–20 at the time, who witnessed many years of parental conflict and continued to live at home. Respondent 20's parents separated when she was aged 0–4 following her father's imprisonment; unaware of these circumstances until much later she was adamant that she did not want contact with her father and would not allow him to have contact with her child.

These accounts were in contrast to Respondent 13 who lost contact with his father at the age of 10 and struggled with the knowledge that his father was 'thousands of miles away' and that his mother was 'struggling for money'. Contact was renewed after a couple of years which he saw as a positive development, possibly influencing his high level of acceptance of post-separation changes.

Respondent 34 was the only respondent to maintain contact with both parents. His parents separated as he started university about 18 months earlier; his situation is described earlier (page 74).

Table 4.2: Respondents who lacked continuity across Continuum 1 and Continuum 2

Respondent ID Number	Continuum 1 – level of satisfaction	Continuum 2 – level of acceptance
13	Medium	High
20	Low	Medium
24	Medium	High
34	Medium	High

Note: Number = 4

Influences on levels of accommodation

Having assessed respondent's levels of accommodation of parental separation and post-separation changes, these became the central category for further analysis of their accounts. The process involving three stages was described in Chapter Three, but it is reiterated here for ease of reference.

The first stage involved using emergent themes from the literature review as a lens through which to view and interpret accounts. These were parental communication with children; children's involvement in decision-making; continuity in post-separation relationships; parental support; children's experience of parental conflict; post-separation family transitions and looking back on childhood experiences of parental separation.

The second stage involved using my professional experience as a further lens through which the data could be interpreted and understood. Previous work as a Family Court Advisor reinforced a number of themes identified in the literature review in particular, the importance of parental communication with children about separation and post-separation arrangements, continuity in post-separation relationships and the impact of parental conflict. Engaging in a 'dialectical dance' moving 'back and forth' between 'experience' and 'abstraction' provided a rich understanding of respondent's lived experiences, allowing common themes, aspects of experience and factors influencing current levels of accommodation to be identified (Finlay, 2009, 10). Used as lenses, these processes allowed trends to be noted, aspects of experience to be highlighted and associations identified.

The third stage of analysis took common themes emerging from respondent's accounts and probed them, noting where clusters of meaning occurred, linking different factors and experiences (Cohen et al, 2011). Individual variations were noted and checked to see whether they were unique or attributable to a group of respondents and could therefore contribute to a greater understanding of the different variables in children's experience. Through this process, clusters of meaning and linkages between themes allowed factors and experiences influencing respondents' levels of accommodation to be identified.

Particular themes emerged as universal aspects of children's experience influencing their current level of accommodation of parental separation, these were:

1. reactions: their response and family members' responses to the separation and changes;
2. support: availability of support and the opportunity to talk to someone about the separation;
3. communication: quality of parental communication at the time of parental separation and whether their views were taken into consideration in post-separation arrangements;
4. conflict: the experience of parental conflict.

Experiences tended to be clustered according to whether young adults showed a high, medium or low level of accommodation of parental separation. While some respondents described experiences which were clearly negative in nature, in some instances the influence of other factors ameliorated their effects, leading to a higher level of accommodation than might otherwise be expected. Understanding children's experiences in such contexts showed how certain factors could encourage a higher level of accommodation over time. Factors such as good communication and support from parent(s), with the opportunity to maintain contact with them after separation were seen as highly significant. In contrast, the presence of parental conflict, poor communication with parents or loss of contact with the non-resident parent after separation, led to a lower level. To understand children's experiences and make sense of the complex interplay of various factors and influences, a new framework for understanding children's accommodation of parental separation and post-separation changes was constructed.

Constructing a new framework for understanding children's accommodation

This part of the chapter outlines the new framework and explains how it creates a deeper understanding of factors and experiences influencing children's accommodation of parental separation and post-separation changes. It should be read alongside the framework which can be found in Appendix Six.

Using levels of accommodation as the central phenomenon around which clusters of meaning and linkages could be recognised, factors and experiences influencing individual respondent's levels of accommodation were identified. Differences emerged between the levels in relation to respondents' reactions, availability of support, opportunity to talk about the separation, parental communication and the presence of parental conflict.

The framework for understanding children's accommodation of parental separation and post-separation changes identifies those factors and experiences influencing levels of accommodation. The main themes emerging from respondents' accounts are identified on the axes. Working inwards from the outer edge of the framework they are: reactions, support/talking, communication and conflict. Each segment of the circle reflects a level of accommodation, reading clockwise starting with the right-hand segment these are: high level of accommodation (green sector), medium level of accommodation (yellow sector) and low level of accommodation (red sector).

When reading the framework, the factors and experiences in each sector indicate the likelihood of this level of accommodation being reached, so if a respondent's account included all factors in the sector there was a greater likelihood that they would show this level of accommodation. For example, if a child experienced minimal changes, was able to maintain contact with both parents and their friendship group, felt supported by both parents, was able to talk to them and felt that his or her views were taken into consideration in post-separation changes, he or she was more likely to have a high level of accommodation. This was the case even where there was evidence of parental conflict or domestic violence, so long as this came to an end when their parents separated.

Their experience was in contrast to those who showed a medium level of accommodation, where contact with one parent was often lost leading to a sense of divided loyalties, particularly where children were aware of the resident parent's dislike of that parent, meaning that they were unable to mention them at home. These children were often isolated with few sources of support and no opportunity to talk to anyone about the separation, although occasionally a resident parent was identified as a source of support. Few learned of the separation in advance and they did not see their needs taken into account in the changes that took place after separation. Over time they tended to develop emotional 'distance' from the separation.

Parental conflict was a feature of some children's experience in the sector showing a low level of accommodation. In these cases, conflict continued to the present day and affected many aspects of their everyday lives. Parents tended to be preoccupied with their own issues rather than attending to their children's needs, and when witnessing arguments at contact handovers older children felt 'caught in the middle' and responsible for younger siblings. In these cases, the clustering of experiences influenced by the presence of parental conflict was seen to exacerbate the respondent's situation, resulting in a low level of accommodation. The interrelatedness of such experiences illustrates how factors cannot be viewed in isolation, but form part of the wider picture of children's experience of family life.

When reading the framework, it should be held in mind that these factors and experiences are indicators of a level of accommodation rather than determinants of a child's accommodation of parental separation and post-separation changes. Certain factors and experiences were seen to modify, ameliorate or sometimes exacerbate the influence of another, thereby affecting a respondent's overall level of accommodation.

For example, loss of contact with the non-resident parent was a factor usually associated with a medium level of accommodation, but where this was what the respondent wanted, it resulted in a high level of accommodation. In other examples where a grandmother took on the mothering role, meaning that a respondent lived with their grandparents, it could bring about stability, resulting in a high level of accommodation. These changes indicate where children thought their views were taken into consideration and/or felt well supported by other family members, the negative impact of loss of contact could be reduced.

In using the axes to read about and understand each cluster of experiences one area cannot be privileged over another, for example reactions cannot be seen as more important than parental communication or the availability of support. There is one notable exception, which is the experience of parental conflict. Where conflict ended after parents separated even if this took a little time, respondents showed a medium or high level of accommodation, but where it continued to the present day, respondents without exception showed a low level of accommodation of parental separation and post-separation changes.

Understanding the new framework

The factors influencing children's accommodation of parental separation and post-separation changes are identified on the axes within the framework, these are; reactions, support and talking, communication and conflict. They correlate with Chapters Six to Nine on Reactions (Chapter Six), Support (Chapter Seven), Communication (Chapter Eight) and Conflict (Chapter Nine); research findings relating to each of the themes are reported there.

The sectors refer to the different levels of accommodation of parental separation and post-separation changes seen in respondents' accounts – high is green, medium is yellow and low is red. There are two ways of reading the framework. One can read about all the factors and experiences influencing a particular level of accommodation of parental separation and post-separation changes by reading all the segments within one sector; so reading all the segments in the green sector shows those factors influencing a high level of accommodation, reading all the segments in the yellow sector shows those influencing a medium level and reading all the segments in the red sector shows those influencing a low level of accommodation. This enables the reader to gain a comprehensive overview of the experiences commonly seen in the accounts of those respondents showing that particular level of accommodation.

The second way to read the framework is to identify one of the themes on the axes and follow that theme round the circle to understand how that particular aspect of children's experience of parental separation influenced the different levels of accommodation. For example, in looking at 'reactions', it can be seen that respondents who showed a high level of accommodation experienced fewer post-separation changes, enabling them to maintain contact with both parents and existing friendship groups. Whereas those who had a medium level of accommodation often lost contact with their non-resident parent after separation, leading to a sense of divided loyalty and emotional distancing over time. Their experience contrasts with those whose parents were preoccupied with their own issues and failed to take account of their child's needs in post-separation arrangements. These respondents tended to have a low level of accommodation.

The framework shows those with a high level of accommodation often identified both parents as sources of support at the time of separation, where only one parent was identified it was their resident parent. Many had access to support within the extended family, usually grandmothers and most were able to talk to someone within their family about the separation commonly parent(s), grandmothers or siblings, but some also spoke to friends. In contrast, those who showed a medium level of accommodation had access to fewer sources of support, they seldom identified anyone within the family and identified none outside the family. These children could be very isolated at the time of parental separation, particularly where they lacked the opportunity to talk to anyone about the changes that were taking place and were unable to identify any source of support. In such cases respondents were likely to show a medium level of accommodation and often indicated that they would have liked the opportunity to talk to someone about what was happening in their family. Respondents who showed a low level of accommodation often identified both parents as sources of support, but this was in the context of high levels of parental conflict, raising questions about the interpretation and understanding of 'support'. Friends were important to those in this level, particularly as they were unable to talk to anyone within their family about the separation. In some instances, children talked to social workers about the separation. This was when parents were unable to agree post-separation arrangements, and the matter was before the Family Courts. Across the levels the number of sources of support or people a child could talk to did not influence their level of accommodation, it was access to at least one source of support within the family, including their resident parent, that was important.

Children who experienced good communication with their parents were usually told of their parents' separation in advance, had their views taken into account in post-separation arrangements and were able to maintain contact with their non–resident parent; they showed a high level of accommodation of the separation and post-separation changes. Their experiences were in marked contrast to those who showed a medium level of accommodation, few of whom learned about the separation in advance and most of whom lost contact with their non-resident parent after separation; they did not see their needs being taken into account in post-separation arrangements. The opportunity to maintain contact with their non-resident parent was highly significant in respondents' accounts and affected their level of accommodation. Those who showed a low level of accommodation experienced difficult communication with their parents, either because parental conflict continued after separation or because separation was a recent event and arrangements were still being decided. This meant that the respondent faced particular uncertainty about arrangements which influenced their level of accommodation.

Where parental conflict continued to the present day, it was a prominent feature in respondents' accounts and resulted in a low level of accommodation. These respondents described how their parents' arguments were a regular feature of contact handovers, they often felt 'caught in the middle' of their parents' arguments and responsible for younger siblings. In contrast, those who experienced parental conflict but lost contact with their non-resident parent after separation were aware of their resident parent's strong dislike of the other and felt 'silenced' from talking about them at home; they had a medium level of accommodation. Where parental conflict or domestic violence featured in the accounts of those with a high level of accommodation, it came to an end when their parents separated, bringing an immediate sense of relief and a high level of accommodation of parental separation and post-separation changes over time.

In the following chapters each of the themes identified on the axes within the framework are considered in turn. The context for these considerations is set in Chapter Five (Setting the context for the framework: emotions) where we listen to what young adults had to say about their initial response to their parents' separation. Their emotional responses were influenced by age and the ability to understand what was happening, therefore their 'voices' are reported according to respondents' ages at the time of separation.

FIVE

Setting the context for the framework: emotions

Case study:

Emily's story

Emily (Respondent 12) is 19 years old, her parents separated recently, just after she moved to another city to study at university. Her mother told her about the separation a few weeks before her father left the family home. She explained:

> 'this has only just happened to me and I am very shocked. They seemed happy enough when I came to university in September so I don't know what has happened while I have been away. I am an only child so there is no one else to talk to about what has changed.'

She described her initial feelings as 'very sad' and 'shocked' and how she 'worries about how things will be in the future...'everything is so strained and sad at home.'

She moved to university in September and lives in halls:

> 'but when I go home at Christmas only Mum will be there. I will see Dad but he is living in a rented flat so it will be very strange.'

She was able to talk to her friends about the separation but having moved away from her home town she said

> 'It is difficult because I have just moved to *** and so I've left my friends at home behind. I have mentioned it to some of the friends I have made while I have been here but it's hard because they don't know me well.'

She described how her parents' separation had affected her ability to concentrate:

> 'I have found it difficult to do my work and to settle in halls since I heard they were separating. I feel like I should be at home but my parents want

me to continue with my university life. I wonder if they were ever happily married or just waiting for me to leave home.'

She was thinking 'of going to see a counsellor if I don't feel any better after Christmas' because she would be able 'to get advice and support which is independent and confidential'.

Emily had a low level of accommodation.

This chapter describes children's initial emotional responses on finding out that their parents were separating, in doing so it sets the context for understanding the themes emerging from their accounts which are considered in detail in the following chapters on reactions, support, communication and parental conflict. Their age at the time of separation influenced their awareness and ability to understand what was happening within the family and to make sense of events, therefore the chapter reports children's emotional responses according to their age at the time of separation using the following age groups; early years (0–4 years), middle childhood (5–8 years), late childhood (9–12 years), teenage years (13–16 years) and late teenage years (17–20 years).

Knowing the changes which children experienced as a result of parental separation provided a context for understanding their experience and emotional responses. Therefore, changes they experienced in terms of with whom they lived, their living arrangements or school they attended (Questions 9 and 10) are identified alongside their thoughts and feelings about the separation and post-separation changes at the time (Questions 8 and 14). This information is provided alongside individual comments which are identified according to their respondent ID number and age at time of separation.

Accounts were scrutinised to glean further information about their initial responses. Contact with non-resident parents emerged as an important issue for some children. Where respondents commented on this it is in reference to contact in the immediate aftermath of their parents' separation in this chapter. Long-term contact arrangements are considered in Chapter Eight (Communication). Some respondents (1, 5, 10, 17, 19, 21, 28, 31) referred to parental conflict in their initial response, their comments are included in this chapter but more detailed consideration can be found in Chapter Nine (Conflict).

The chapter started with Emily's story. She was one of the respondents in this study who experienced parental separation as a young adult, her parents' separation coinciding with her move to study at a university in another city and to independent living. Her case highlights some of the issues which young adults face in this situation.

The chapter concludes with discussion of the range of initial emotions children expressed about their parents' separation and the influence that their age, life transitions and parental conflict had on their experience.

Early years (0–4 years)

Seven respondents (6, 7, 18, 20, 22, 27, 30) were in their early years at the time of their parents' separation. Their characteristics, including current age, gender and level of accommodation of parental separation, can be found in Table 5.1.

Not all of the respondents described their first thoughts and feelings, but those who did said either that they were too young to understand what was happening (6, 18, 30) or that they could not remember.

As Respondent 30 explained:

> 'I can't remember. I was too young so I only know what I have been told.' (Respondent 30; aged 0–4)

Two (6, 18) recalled it being an 'upsetting' time but did not elaborate. After separation they lived with their mother and brothers. After separation they lived with their mother and brothers, there were no indications of further changes.

Another respondent (22), however, recalled resenting her mother after her father left the family home.

Table 5.1: Characteristics of respondents in their early years at the time of separation

Respondent number	Age at time of separation	Current age	Gender	Level of accommodation
6	0–4 years	19	Female	High
7	0–4 years	23	Female	High
18	0–4 years	19	Female	High
20	0–4 years	30	Female	Lacked continuity
22	0–4 years	25	Female	Medium
27	0–4 years	18	Female	High
30	0–4 years	18	Female	High

Note: Number = 7

'I just know that I resented my mum. I think I took my frustration out on her as she was the parent we lived with.' (Respondent 22; aged 0–4)

She lived with her brother, mother and mother's new partner after separation. As the resident parent her mother bore the brunt of her frustration. Her experience is described in more detail in the case study of Gemma, in Chapter Six (Reactions).

One respondent (27), rather than focusing on the initial separation, described the emotional impact of growing up without a father in her life:

'My parents had already split up so it was hard growing up without a dad. Dad's never been part of my life. Mum does not say much about it other than he could not be trusted to look after me properly – I think there are some medical issues but I am not sure what they are. She has never spoken badly about my dad.' (Respondent 27; aged 0–4)

While parental separation is an event, the process of separation and putting post-separation arrangements in place often extends over a long period and is subject to review as children's needs change. These respondents experienced parental separation at least 14 years ago, for some it was seen as a distant event in their lives, whereas for others it continued to exert considerable influence on their lives, as can be seen in their reactions, described in the next chapter.

Middle childhood (5–8 years)

Five respondents (4, 15, 16, 23, 25) were in middle childhood at the time of their parents' separation, as can be seen in Table 5.2 which shows population data and their level of accommodation.

These respondents described many emotions on hearing of their parents' separation: they tended to feel sad, upset, angry, scared, confused and stressed. It was a confusing as well as an emotional time and many expressed a mix of emotions, often feeling upset or sad as well as an inability to understand the situation.

One (23) described how she was:

'upset and scared because I was only young, so did not fully understand why they were separating.' (Respondent 23; aged 5–8)

Table 5.2: Characteristics of respondents in middle childhood at the time of separation

Respondent number	Age at time of separation	Current age	Gender	Level of accommodation
4	5–8 years	19	Female	High
15	5–8 years	21	Female	High
16	5–8 years	25	Female	Medium
23	5–8 years	20	Female	High
25	5–8 years	19	Female	High

Note: Number = 5

Her response was to try to make her parents stay together:

> 'Because I was young I saw it in a simple way and pleaded with my mum not to leave Dad.' (Respondent 23; aged 5–8)

Post-separation arrangements meant that she lived with her mother and sister, moved house and school and had to adjust to seeing her father at specific times.

A sense of blame featured in most accounts, with some children thinking that it was something they or their siblings had done that had caused the separation (4, 15, 16), others blamed one of their parents (4, 25). Many referred to their confusion or lack of understanding about what was happening in their family at that time.

Respondent 4 described how initially she

> 'was very upset and a bit angry and I think I felt that my siblings and I had done something to cause all this.' (Respondent 4; aged 5–8)

She went on to explain how she continued to feel:

> 'confused and blamed Mum for letting Dad leave'. (Respondent 4; aged 5–8)

After separation she lived with her mother, brother and sister.

Initially Respondent 15 believed that her parents' separation was her fault; she responded by trying

> 'to pretend it wasn't happening by not thinking about it'. (Respondent 15; aged 5–8)

But as changes took place involving her moving to live with her mother and grandparents she felt 'sad' and

> 'didn't understand the situation because I was so young. I started to feel resentment towards my mother for letting my dad leave.' (Respondent 15; aged 5–8)

For Respondent 16 it was the second time that she had experienced parental separation, her parents separated when she 'was too young to remember', and she had 'gone to live with grandparents', then she experienced her grandparents' separation. She explained how

> 'when Grandad left I realised it would all change…like a lot of children I felt like it was my fault and I had to get used to changes. Now I look back and think I was lucky in some ways, with two loving grandparents.' (Respondent 16; aged 5–8)

After separation she lived with her grandmother.

Respondent 25 blamed her mother (resident parent) for the separation, describing that

> '[I] hated my mum for making my dad leave.' (Respondent 25; aged 5–8)

Her parents' separation brought about many changes, including moving house and school and her father's 'new girlfriend' being part of her life. She described feeling stressed and as the oldest child feeling

> 'responsible for my brother and I worried about him a lot. When I think back I was very stressed and I was upset easily and started to pull my hair out which became a habit.' (Respondent 25; aged 5–8)

These respondents experienced parental separation at least a decade ago and so had had some time to adjust to their parents living separately and the changes that this brought.

Late childhood (9–12 years)

The largest group of respondents, 15 (1, 2, 3, 5, 8, 10, 11, 13, 14, 17, 21, 26, 28, 31, 32), experienced parental separation in late childhood, their population data and level of accommodation can be seen in Table 5.3. Like the children in middle childhood, these respondents described a mix of emotions on learning of their parents' separation. They often expressed upset, anger, sometimes they were concerned that it was something they had done that brought this about, sometimes they blamed one parent but an additional feature in some accounts was worry about the future and anxiety about what would happen. A particular feature of some male accounts was frustration about post-separation changes and the painful loss of contact with their father. Many respondents (1, 5, 10, 17, 21, 28, 31) identified parental conflict as a feature of their experience.

Table 5.3: Characteristics of respondents in late childhood at the time of separation

Respondent number	Age at time of separation	Current age	Gender	Level of accommodation
1	9–12 years	18	Female	Low
2	9–12 years	27	Female	Low
3	9–12 years	19	Male	High
5	9–12 years	18	Male	Medium
8	9–12 years	20	Female	High
10	9–12 years	18	Female	High
11	9–12 years	20	Female	High
13	9–12 years	18	Male	Lacked continuity
14	9–12 years	20	Male	High
17	9–12 years	19	Female	Low
21	9–12 years	18	Female	High
26	9–12 years	19	Female	High
28	9–12 years	23	Female	Medium
31	9–12 years	19	Female	High
32	9–12 years	22	Male	Medium

Note: Number = 15

Respondents were often upset when finding out that their parents were separating

'I couldn't stop crying and didn't know what to do, it was like a panic.' (Respondent 1; aged 9–12)

'I thought the sky had fallen in. I was quite religious and I wanted God to make it all better.' (Respondent 17; aged 9–12)

When they were unclear about adult's motives for leaving, children could think they were to blame for the separation. Following her parents' separation, Respondent 2 moved to live with her grandparents who then separated, she described how she

'was very angry [when] Dad moved to live with another woman and her children. I also thought it might be something I had done that made him go and it was my fault. Then when I was 11 I went to live with Nana and Grandad and that was fine until he left as well. He told me he was going on the day but I never understood why.' (Respondent 2; aged 9–12)

She went on to say

'I thought it was my fault in some way I think a lot of children think that.' (Respondent 2; aged 9–12)

Sometimes children saw one parent as responsible for the separation and blamed that parent, such as Respondent 31 who lived with her mother, sister and stepfather after separation

'I was devastated and blamed Mum at first for breaking the family up. It was like my world had collapsed.' (Respondent 31; aged 9–12)

She went on to explain how

'Moving house was horrible and I just did not settle. Again, I thought it was all Mum's fault.' (Respondent 31; aged 9–12)

Others held both parents responsible for the separation and associated changes:

'I didn't know why this had happened and I was confused and annoyed with my parents for letting it happen.' (Respondent 32; aged 9–12)

He expressed his

'frustration and anger at changes happening.' (Respondent 32; aged 9–12)

After separation he lived with his mother, stepfather and siblings, moved house and changed school.

Some respondents worried about the future, how they might cope and what was going to happen, which created particular anxiety:

'I didn't know how I was going to cope.' (Respondent 11; aged 9–12)

She lived with her mother, stepfather and brother after separation, moving house to do so.

Respondent 3 expressed similar anxieties. She lived with her father and stepmother after separation:

'I didn't really understand what was happening. I was upset and worried about what was going to happen.' (Respondent 3; aged 9–12)

Respondent 14 also said that he

'didn't really understand what was going on.' (Respondent 14; aged 9–12)

He felt

'sad and upset because I didn't know what would happen.' (Respondent 14; aged 9–12)

After separation he lived with his father.

Two male respondents (5, 13) described their feelings about the loss of contact with their father:

'It was hard not seeing Dad or hearing from him.' (Respondent 5; aged 9–12)

'It was hard for me because I was 10 years old and my dad didn't see me for two years.' (Respondent 13; aged 9–12)

Where parental separation brought about an end to parental conflict, however, respondents' initial feelings were of relief. Their accounts are discussed in more detail in Chapter Nine.

'In the end it was a relief because of the way Dad behaved at home.' (Respondent 10; aged 9–12)

'In a way I was happier because of my dad being violent towards Mum.' (Respondent 21; aged 9–12)

'Relief and safe.' (Respondent 28; aged 9–12)

These respondents faced transition from primary to secondary school around the same time as their parents' separation, and so faced a number of life changes at this time. Where there was confusion or lack of knowledge about the separation and post-separation arrangements, children faced anxiety and upset, sometimes leading to anger and frustration. When faced with a number of changes, in the people with whom they lived, where they lived and the school they attended, children could experience considerable anxiety and question their ability to cope.

Teenage years (13–16 years)

Four respondents (9, 19, 29, 33) experienced parental separation in their teenage years, their population data and level of accommodation can be found in Table 5.4.

Table 5.4: Characteristics of respondents in early teenage years at the time of separation

Respondent number	Age at time of separation	Current age	Gender	Level of accommodation
9	13–16 years	19	Female	High
19	13–16 years	19	Female	High
29	13–16 years	27	Male	High
33	13–16 years	30	Female	Medium

Note: Number = 4

The initial responses of respondents in this age group varied considerably between respondents who were taken by surprise by the event (33) and those who had experienced their parents' separation previously and anticipated a recurrence (9, 19). Respondents often referred to their own coping abilities.

Respondent (33) described her shock on learning about her parents' separation

> 'My first response was devastation – I couldn't believe it was happening.' (Respondent 33; aged 13–16)

Coping with all the changes it brought, alongside studying for GCSE exams, she recalls it being a difficult time, the resulting pressure eventually leading her to become unwell:

> 'Even though it was less stressful at home [after separation] I was not coping well with all the changes and my GCSEs at the same time. I eventually got ill.' (Respondent 33; aged 13–16)

In contrast, Respondent 9 was unsurprised by the news her parents were separating because they had separated twice before, but she described her upset on realising their separation was permanent this time:

> 'I knew it was coming so I wasn't surprised. They'd separated twice before so I kind of knew what to expect. I was still upset though because I thought, "This time it's actually happening and they're never getting back together again."' (Respondent 9; aged 13–16)

Respondent 19's parents had also separated previously but she realised that:

> 'This time was different and I knew it was going to be permanent.' (Respondent 19; aged 13–16)

They adopted particular coping strategies to protect themselves, Respondent 9 referring to how she would:

> 'bottle up my thoughts and feelings and not talk about it because if I started talking I worried I would not stop. I

would say too much and upset people.' (Respondent 9; aged 13–16)

Respondent 19 said that:

'I used to just say "I don't know" when people asked how I was. I didn't know what to say without upsetting people so I didn't say much at all. It was easier to try to distance myself from it all.' (Respondent 19; aged 13–16)

In protecting others, she sought to create emotional distance for herself. Parental conflict was a feature of her account.

The remaining respondent (29) struggled to remember his initial thoughts and feelings on learning of his parents' separation, he suggested that this was probably by choice, giving indications that he attempted to distance himself from the experience deliberately

'I can't remember – probably chose not to.' (Respondent 29; aged 13–16)

He explained how after his father left, his grandmother moved to live with him, his mother and his siblings.

'I just don't remember but I think it was worse for the others, my older brother was very hurt and still is I think.' (Respondent 29; aged 13–16)

As teenagers, these respondents had a clearer understanding of what their parents' separation might mean and how it might have an impact on their lives. They were able to exercise increasing agency in their own lives, for example through the coping abilities they chose to employ in terms of to whom they might speak, or not, about their home situation.

Late teenage years (17–20 years)

Three respondents (12, 24, 34) experienced parental separation in their late teenage years, their population data and level of accommodation can be seen in Table 5.5.

Two respondents (12, 34) experienced parental separation after they left home to attend university; this was a very recent event and it was evident from their accounts that they were still adjusting to the changes it brought at the same time as adjusting to living independently at

Table 5.5: Characteristics of respondents in late teenage years at the time of separation

Respondent number	Age at time of separation	Current age	Gender	Level of accommodation
12	17–20 years	19	Female	Low
24	17–20 years	27	Female	Lacked continuity
34	17–20 years	20	Male	Lacked continuity

Note: Number = 3

university in another town. Emily's situation (12), described in the case study at the beginning of the chapter, explained how experiencing parental separation at the same time as starting university in a different city brought particular challenges. She described her shock and worry about 'how things will be in the future' reflecting the rawness of emotion at this stage. She explained how not living at home and hearing about their separation only after she left, meant that she lacked full understanding of what had happened and the changes that were taking place, which created particular anxieties.

Respondent 34 had been in a similar position the previous year when his parents separated in his first year of university:

> 'I wish it hadn't happened but Mum and Dad seem happier now they live separate lives.' (Respondent 34; aged 17–20)

In his account, he explained the difficulties in maintaining contact with both of them given the distance involved in travelling between his university accommodation and home area where they continued to live. Some adjustments continued to be made, but overall:

> 'Dad and I have grown closer which is good.' (Respondent 34; aged 17–20)

The remaining respondent (24) experienced parental separation when she was 17 years old. Parental conflict was a feature of her parents' relationship and the relief brought about by their separation was palpable.

> 'At last, they should have done it years ago! Life was so much better.' (Respondent 24; aged 17–20)

When asked to say a little more about her thoughts and feelings at the time, she said:

'I was just relieved that it was all over now and we could finally start living.' (Respondent 24; aged 17–20)

Respondents experiencing parental separation and transitioning to university life and independent living simultaneously faced a number of life changes in a short period of time. Living away from home in a new area having not done so before and adjusting to the demands of studying at higher education level created its own challenges. They lacked knowledge about what was happening in their parents' relationships and the arrangements being put in place, which gave rise to considerable anxiety as evidenced elsewhere in their accounts.

Discussion

Range of emotions

When describing their initial thoughts and feelings on hearing that their parents were separating, respondents referred to a range of emotions. Often there was sadness, sometimes shock, in many cases upset and confusion and in some instances anger and frustration. Many described a mix of emotions, sometimes tinged with anxiety about what would happen next, this was particularly evident among those in late childhood at the time of separation.

Those in middle (5–8 years) or late childhood (9–12 years) often framed their emotional response within a blame narrative thinking that they may be to blame for the separation or maybe that what they and/or their siblings had done might have caused this event. Left uncorrected these misapprehensions had the potential to affect their adjustment and accommodation of parental separation and post-separation changes.

Those in their teenage years at the time of their parents' separation had a clearer understanding of what this might mean and the changes it was likely to bring; they were also able to exercise increased agency in their lives. Nonetheless, when parental separation coincided with other events or transitions in their lives, such as studying for GCSEs or leaving home to attend university, children faced a number of challenges within a short period of time and experienced a more difficult adjustment (Flowerdew and Neale, 2003).

Age and transitions

Children's age at the time of parental separation affected their ability to recall their initial thoughts and feelings about the event with those in their early years unable to recall their parents' separation, although one respondent (22) remembered many post-separation changes and the resentment which she felt towards her mother, the resident parent, as a result.

Children in middle childhood (5–8 years) described feeling sad, upset, angry or scared and confused by their parents' separation. Confusion was often created by a lack of information about what was happening alongside their limited ability to understand the situation. Experiencing parental separation for a second time could be particularly confusing and raised questions for children about whether they were to blame in some way (see Respondents 2 and 16's accounts). Such experiences gave rise to a sense of 'difference' from other children and self doubt, emphasising the need for explanations to be given more than once and reinforced by people trusted by the child (Butler et al, 2002; Maes et al, 2011).

Children in late childhood (aged 9–12 years) at the time of separation described similar emotions to those in middle childhood. Many had an understanding of why their parents were separating, which could be related to their increased age and ability to understand, to explanations being provided by parents, to the higher incidence of parental conflict within this group, or a combination of these factors. Among the male respondents in this age group, loss of contact with their father was a loss that was keenly felt (5, 13, 32) (Butler et al, 2002). When compounded by other changes that were taking place, it could lead to frustration and anger with parents for letting this happen (32).

These children experienced the transition from primary to secondary school at the same time as their parents' separation and post-separation arrangements being put in place, leading some children to experience a number of significant changes within a relatively short time period. A lack of information about was happening in their family situation created additional anxiety about the future, sometimes raising questions for the child about how they would cope (11).

Where this occurred, accounts had similarities with those in the oldest age group who experienced parental separation alongside the transition to higher education and described their initial shock on learning about the separation and anxiety about what was going to happen in the future. Moving away from home to live independently and continue their academic studies gave rise to a particular set of emotions and challenges (Abetz and Wang, 2017), highlighting the continuing need for parental explanation as children reach adulthood. In these cases, there was evidence of the pace and 'cumulative "weight"' of these experiences affecting respondents' levels of accommodation of parental separation and post-separation changes (Flowerdew and Neale, 2003, 157).

Increased understanding of what their parents' separation might mean and how it could affect their lives was evident in the accounts of those who were teenagers at the time of separation. They were able to exercise increasing agency in their lives and the desire to create some emotional distance – by trying to forget or control how much they talked to others about the separation – was a common theme.

Where parental separation brought about an end to parental conflict, children viewed their parents' separation positively from the outset. This was a consistent theme across all age groups and is considered in more detail in Chapter Nine (Conflict).

The following chapters enable the reader to develop a more detailed understanding of children's experiences of parental separation, in particular their reactions to the separation, the availability of support and opportunity to talk to someone, the quality of parental communication and the impact of parent conflict. These experiences emerged from respondent's accounts as influential factors in their level of accommodation. It would be useful to refer to the framework for understanding children's accommodation of parental separation (Appendix Six) when reading Chapters Six to Nine.

The next chapter focuses on children's reactions to their parents' separation and the changes it introduced into their lives. It takes account of family members' responses to these events, particularly those of parents and siblings, because these had an impact on children's experiences influencing their level of accommodation.

SIX

Reactions

Case study:
Gemma's story

Gemma (Respondent 22) aged 25 years old, was 0–4 years old when her parents separated. After viewing the PSV and reflecting on her experience, she explained:

> 'Looking at the clip, I can see that some things are similar, but the situation was different. When I look back I realise that there were lots of problems at home and I didn't really get on with Mum or Dad properly. I thought Dad didn't want us when he left and I wanted him to notice us. I thought Mum should have done more to keep it together. My brother reacted by always [being] in trouble at school and with the police. If I hadn't gone to live with grandparents when I started secondary school I don't know what would have happened. I still get a bit jealous of other people when they get on with their families, even though my family is better now than it was. I still have little contact with Mum and Dad. I have tried to make sure I don't make the same mistakes my mum and dad did and I give my children lots of attention.'

Following her parents' separation she lived with her brother and mother who 'moved her partner in with us and then soon after we moved to his house'. She remembered 'not getting on with my mum at the time. I thought it was her fault', and taking her 'frustration out on her as she was the parent we lived with'.

The separation and post-separation changes were 'never discussed and I was not asked what I thought. I think they thought I was too young'. Her grandmother was a source of support and she moved to live with her grandparents when she was 11. She spoke to a counsellor about her family situation, but did not comment on when, who arranged it or her thoughts on the experience.

She described other family members' responses, in particular how her brother:

'became aggressive and violent, he was suspended from school and eventually expelled. He also got in with a gang and got into trouble with the police. He has served two prison sentences.'

And how her 'mum couldn't stand Dad's new partner's children and tried to insist that we did not see them when we saw him, which led to lots of arguments.'

She would have liked the opportunity 'to have ongoing help and support [because] I was going through a lot [and] it would help to know that lots of people go through the same sort of things'. Nonetheless she thought her experience had made her 'the person I am today', she was 'determined to be a good role model, wife and mother' and to make sure she listened 'to my children and prioritise their needs so that they do not have the same experiences as me'.

She recognised that 'each family is different' but thought that:

'people need support and maybe classes about getting married and how to bring up children. That would mean that the children get listened to instead of it being all about the adults.'

Gemma had a medium level of accommodation.

Children's initial reactions to their parents' separation was one of the themes to emerge from analysis of young adults' accounts and is the focus of this chapter. The chapter describes how children reacted to their parents' separation and the changes it brought to their lives. Some respondents referred to parental conflict in their accounts, their comments are reported in this chapter but their experience is discussed in more detail in Chapter Nine. It takes account of other family members' responses to these events, particularly those of parents and siblings, because often these had an impact on children's experiences. The chapter discusses how children's reactions and other family members' responses influenced levels of accommodation of parental separation over time.

Understanding children's reactions involved examining accounts to ascertain their views on what changed in their lives immediately after they realised that their parents were separating (Question 11) and knowing with whom they lived and any changes they experienced in living arrangements or school after separation (Questions 9 and 10). Having watched the PSV, respondents were asked to reflect on their own experiences, in particular whether there were any similarities between the PSV and their own experience of parental separation (Question 6), analysis of these responses often yielded further information about their reactions. Other family members' responses often had an impact on children's reactions (Question 16) so these were taken into consideration when examining respondents' accounts. The level of accommodation shown by respondents is noted by inclusion of the word 'high', 'medium', 'low' or 'lacked continuity' after their respondent ID number.

In line with Chapter Five, in order to understand children's reactions and build a picture of individual responses, children's reactions are reported according to their age. The chapter discusses how children's reactions and other family members' responses influenced individual levels of accommodation of parental separation. As can be seen in the framework, higher levels of accommodation were recorded where post-separation changes were minimised and children were able to maintain relationships with both parents and their friendship group.

The chapter started with Gemma's story, she was a respondent in her early years (0–4) at the time of separation. Her account shows that her parents' separation brought about a number of changes: her father left the family home, her mother moved her new partner into the household and they moved house. Contact with her father involved his new partner and her children, leading to conflict between her parents, an aspect of her experience which is considered in more detail in Chapter Nine. When she reached secondary school age, she moved to live with her grandparents. Her academic success is in marked contrast to her brother's school experience which involved suspensions (fixed-term exclusions) and eventual expulsion (permanent exclusion). She refers to the impact her early experiences have had on her adult life.

Early years (0–4 years)

Respondents (6, 7, 18, 20, 22, 27, 30) who experienced parental separation in their early years described a range of separation experiences. Many provided accounts of the changes that took place in their family, describing how parents lived in different homes (6, high; 18, high). Some provided more detailed accounts (20, lacked continuity; 22, medium; 30, high) and it was evident that they had gained a greater understanding of the situation as they got older. Others (6, 18) said that they were too young to understand what was happening, but explained the changes that took place. One respondent (7, high) described the actions of others rather than her reactions, after separation she lived with her mother and

'Mum's new partner who got drunk and caused trouble when he came home late.' (Respondent 7; aged 0–4)

One (27, high) continued to focus on the emotional impact of growing up without a father, her view was open to a number of interpretations:

'My view is dads change.' (Respondent 27; aged 0–4)

In describing their reactions it was evident that they were unaware of the reasons for their parents' separation until a much later date, as Respondent 20's account (lacked continuity) illustrated. Her parents separated because her father was imprisoned, unaware of this at the time she believed that her father was working away from home, only learning the truth when she was in secondary school; she described her disbelief and upset on hearing this. Who revealed his whereabouts or the reason for his imprisonment is unknown, but her views on any possible contact between her father and her child were unequivocal. She lived with her mother and explained how she

'no longer saw Dad. Now I'm older I know he was in prison but when I was growing up I was told he worked away. That was fine because I could tell my friends in school he had a great job. I found out where he really was when I was in secondary school and someone told me. I didn't believe them at first – then Mum told me the truth and I was really upset for while.' (Respondent 20; aged 0–4)

Contact ended after her parents separated, and now she was a mother she was clear that

'I don't want him near my child either.' (Respondent 20; aged 0–4)

Reliant on what others had told her, Respondent 30 (high) was aware after her parents separated that her mother moved to Egypt with her new partner. As a consequence, she moved with her father to live at his parents' home. She lost direct contact with her mother, as she explained:

'We lived there so they could look after me while he worked. Mum left him for someone else who she eventually married and had children with. He was a student in this country but after he graduated they went to live in his country. I have seen photos of my brothers and sisters but I've not seen Mum since because they live in Egypt.' (Respondent 30; aged 0–4)

She was not the only respondent whose experience of contact was affected by substantial geographical distance (see Respondent 13's account below) but her age at the time of separation meant that she could not 'remember' her 'parents separating' or the time they lived together although she did recall her father being 'very upset at the time'.

Gemma's experience (22, medium) was described in the case study at the start of the chapter. She found it hard to 'think back' to their separation but recalled 'not getting on' with her mother at the time: as the resident parent she held her responsible for the changes that took place. After separation she lived with her mother and brother and experienced many changes in her life with the introduction of mother's new partner to the household, moving house and involvement of father's partner and her children in contact. The lack of explanation left her feeling overlooked and unnoticed when her father left; she thought her parents could have been more attentive to her and her brother's needs.

She described her parents' arguments about contact arrangements (discussed in more detail in Chapter Nine) and how the difficulties in family relationships led her to move to live with her grandparents as she started secondary school. She viewed this as a positive move which had a significant impact on her life, intimating that she may not be where she is now – a university student, wife and mother – if she had not taken this decision. Certainly, her brother's situation stood in marked contrast to her experience.

Reflecting on the PSV, her comments highlighted the profound affect which her parents' separation, subsequent changes and post-separation family situation had on her and how these experiences influence her adult life and the way she views family relationships. In particular, the way in which she parents her children and her determination 'to be a good role model, wife and mother'.

Having experienced parental separation at a young age most of the respondents in this age group have gone on to accept the changes brought about by their parents' separation and showed a high level of accommodation. Interestingly, those that did not, Gemma (22, medium) and Respondent 20 (lacked continuity) were parents, in their reflections their reaction to parental separation was considered in the context of decisions which they were making about their own parenting.

Middle childhood (5–8 years)

Those respondents (4, 15, 16, 23, 25) in middle childhood at the time of their parents' separation, described the changes they experienced and recalled their reactions as well as those of other family members. Arrangements for seeing their non-resident parent were a key feature of their accounts and the need for time to adjust to the changes was emphasised by many, in each case their non-resident parent was their father (grandfather in Respondent 16's case). All had contact after separation, but sometimes it took a while for arrangements to be put in place as in two cases (4, 15).

In one case (4, high), this is what she wanted initially, she lived with her mother and grandparents after separation:

> 'I didn't see Dad. I didn't want to for a long while.' (Respondent 4; aged 5–8)

One (16, medium) experienced separation for a second time; having moved to live with her grandparents following her parents' separation when she was very young, she now faced their separation. Her description of contact arrangements implies that she lost contact with her father:

> 'I was so young I don't really remember but we didn't keep in touch much and I regret that now.' (Respondent 16; aged 5–8)

However, she maintained some contact with her grandfather:

> 'A bit like in the clip. It's like you are letting one parent down if you see the other one so you feel guilty. You want to please them both but you can't.' (Respondent 16; aged 5–8)

Other changes

In some cases, contact was one of a number of changes. Respondent 23 (high) described living with her mother and sister after separation and moving to another part of the city, which involved changing school and

> 'how often I saw my dad. Me and my sister had to adjust to a new school and home.' (Respondent 23; aged 5–8)

Her reaction was similar to one of the girls in the PSV, in that

> 'I used to want to turn the clock back so that we could all be happy again.' (Respondent 23; aged 5–8)

Throughout these changes she drew on the support of her older sister (see the case study of Bethany in Chapter Seven).

Changes sometimes involved not only adjusting to moving between two homes, a new home and new school, but also the introduction of a new partner. It could be

> 'confusing having to live between two homes and my dad had a new girlfriend, so we had to get used to her'. (Respondent 25; aged 5–8)

As the older sister, Respondent 25 (high) remembered the separation and her younger brother's response to their father's new partner.

> 'I remember my parents separating but my little brother was too young to but I do remember he grew to hate my dad's new girlfriend and always played up when we visited him.' (Respondent 25; aged 5–8)

The mix of emotions they felt on learning of their parents' separation (described in the previous chapter) indicated that these children tended to feel sad, upset and confused and often thought it was something they and/or their siblings had done that had brought about the separation, illustrating the need for children of this age to be given clear explanations of what was happening in their family and the likely changes, to dispel their misconceptions.

Those respondents (4, high; 15, high) who experienced a delay in contact arrangements being put in place recalled their parents' emotional reactions:

> 'Mum was very upset all the time.' (Respondent 4; aged 5–8)

> 'Dad drank more and Mum just cried a lot.' (Respondent 15; aged 5–8)

Aware of their parents' responses, these children may have felt unable to ask about what was happening in their family and seek explanation about the loss of contact. It is possible that Respondent 4's awareness of her mother's upset influenced her initial attitude towards contact with her father.

Some children in this age group experienced many changes as a result of their parents' separation, including moving house, moving school and the introduction of a step-parent; nonetheless, over time, they adjusted to the changes and showed a high level of accommodation. Some were aware of their parents' reactions to the separation, which could result in a delay in contact arrangements being put in place. Over time this was addressed, meaning that all children in this age group had contact with their non-resident parent (or grandparent), a factor contributing to a high level of accommodation of parental separation and post-separation changes. Only (16, medium) had a lower level of accommodation; her experience was complicated by it being the second time that she had experienced parental separation: this time it was her grandparents' separation.

Late childhood (9–12 years)

Those aged 9–12 at the time of separation experienced more post-separation changes than other age groups in the study, including living with a step-parent (3, high; 11, high; 31, high; 32 medium) and moving school in one case (32, medium). Their initial reactions tended to focus on the immediate changes and recognition that family relationships would no longer be as they were before. Interestingly, five respondents (1, low; 3, high; 8, high; 14, high; 26, high) lived with their father after separation. Parental conflict featured in nine accounts (1, 2, 5, 10, 11, 17, 21 28, 31) and their experience is considered in more detail in Chapter Nine.

Sometimes respondents provided a general response to what changed in their lives immediately after their parents separated, as seen in the responses of two male respondents:

> 'I knew everything was going to change.' (Respondent 3; aged 9–12)

> 'I knew it was going to be very different from then on.' (Respondent 14; aged 9–12)

Contact

Some children were unable to see one parent for a while after separation. This could be a temporary situation, as in two cases (1, low; 17, low) where respondents lived with their father:

'I didn't see Mum for a while.' (Respondent 1; aged 9–12)

'For a while we hardly saw Mum.' (Respondent 17; aged 9–12)

A high level of parental conflict was identified in each of these accounts and post-separation arrangements were eventually determined by the Family Court.

For others, the lack of contact was long term, in these cases the reactions of other family members had an impact on their experience. Two male respondents, who lost contact with their fathers:

'felt obliged to hate my dad', (Respondent 13; aged 9–12)

or faced the experience of:

'Mum and my sisters were always having a go about Dad and I didn't feel I could mention his name at home.' (Respondent 5; aged 9–12)

Another male respondent (32, medium) did not refer to his father in the rest of his responses, suggesting that contact was lost at this stage. He described how after separation he lived with his mother, stepfather and brother which involved changing school:

'We moved to another area and it messed up school and friends.' (Respondent 32; aged 9–12)

He described how neither he nor his brother liked these changes, but they had different perspectives which he attributed to their different interpretations of events:

'I didn't like what was happening nor did my brother but he accepted that we had a step-father living with us...I had a different view about what had gone on.' (Respondent 32; aged 9–12)

Divided loyalties

It was not unusual for children in this age group to feel anxious, particularly when they experienced parental conflict and the separation involved changes in the people with whom they lived. After separation, Respondent 31 (high) lived with her mother, sister and stepfather, she described her initial reaction:

> 'I was unhappy and cried a lot. I became very anxious.'
> (Respondent 31; aged 9–12)

The PSV resonated with her, reminding her how it felt being 'torn between two parents':

> 'It was very similar and reminded me how difficult it was, seeing the children torn between two parents.' (Respondent 31; aged 9–12)

After separation, another respondent (11, high) lived with her mother, brother and 'stepdad', she referred to the anxiety which she and her brother felt as a result of these changes.

> 'Both my brother and I developed a lot of anxiety.'
> (Respondent 11; aged 9–12)

Feeling divided loyalties between their parents or as they put it 'torn between' two parents was not uncommon, two other respondents (3, high; 14, high) described their experiences in a similar way. Each lived with their father after separation and Respondent 3 lived with his stepmother.

Sibling relationships were put to the test when respondents had different views about post-separation arrangements to their siblings, which could also lead to a sense of divided loyalties, as in the case of one (26, high) who said:

> 'It was hard because my brothers wanted to live with Mum and I wanted to stay with Dad.' (Respondent 26; aged 9–12)

The PSV resonated with her in terms of the discussions she had with her brothers, eventually leading to a decision which meant that they lived with their father and had contact with their mother:

'The case study is very realistic for me because my brothers and I didn't agree at first about where we would live and who we would keep in touch with.' (Respondent 26; aged 9–12)

Another respondent (28, medium) held different views about post-separation arrangements to those of her siblings which led to a situation unique within the study, in which she lived with one parent but apart from her siblings, as she explained:

'When my parents split, I knew what had happened and went with Mum. The younger ones didn't know what had happened and didn't know what Dad had done so they stayed and blamed Mum.' (Respondent 28; aged 9–12)

Her parents had separated twice previously, on each occasion she and her mother moved to live with her grandparents. She described her initial reaction to the separation:

'Although I became more confident with friends at first, I really missed being around my younger siblings so much.' (Respondent 28; aged 9–12)

'It was a bit like in the clip my brother, sister and me all had different views. After he left I realised my family was different to everyone else's and I felt very lonely.' (Respondent 28; aged 9–12)

A further respondent (2, low) described how she had a different view about her parents' separation and post-separation arrangements to those of her siblings, she referred to her father's 'other family' indicating that he had a partner and children elsewhere:

'After I heard about Dad's "other family" I wanted nothing to do with him but my sister wanted to keep both parents happy and tried hard to do so.' (Respondent 2; aged 9–12)

She lived with her grandparents after separation.

Sense of relief

Where respondents identified domestic violence, which came to an end as a result of their parents' separation, their sense of relief was evident. This was the experience of two respondents (10, high; 21, high), who lived with their mothers after separation. Respondent 10 described how she felt

'less scared and more relaxed'. (Respondent 10; aged 9–12)

However,

'because of the way things were it was all kept quiet and my friends were shocked when it came out'. (Respondent 10; aged 9–12)

Referring to the PSV she explained how she

'reacted the same way as the girl did. I knew that it was best if my mum and dad were not together.' (Respondent 10; aged 9–12)

Respondent (21, high) described how when her parents' separated, she

'stopped being frightened at home'. (Respondent 21; aged 9–12)

She saw her reaction as similar to Natasha's in the PSV:

'I reacted the same way as in the film. I knew that it would be better if my mum and dad split up.' (Respondent 21; aged 9–12)

In this age group the loss of contact with their non-resident parent was a key theme, in some cases this was a short-term situation and contact was renewed at a later stage by parents themselves or intervention of the Family Courts (1, low; 17, low), but sometimes it was a permanent loss (32, medium). Where the loss of contact was complicated by parental conflict it had a significant impact on respondents' accommodation of their parents' separation and post-separation changes. The loss of contact with their father was felt very keenly by male respondents (5, 13, 32) in this age group, all of whom showed a medium level of accommodation of parental separation and post-separation changes. A sense of divided loyalties was also a key theme, with some respondents feeling 'torn between parents' as a result of the changes (3, high; 11, high; 14, high; 31, high) and others as a result of their view about the separation and post-separation changes being different to that of their siblings (2, low; 26, high; 28, medium). This could have far reaching implications with siblings living in different households (28, medium) and had a significant impact on respondents' levels of accommodation.

Teenage years (13–16 years)

Respondents (9, 19, 29, 33) in their teenage years at the time of parental separation tended to focus on post-separation arrangements and their attitudes towards them. There was evidence that most had their views taken into account in post-separation arrangements.

Contact

The importance of their relationship with their non-resident parent (father) and desire for contact to continue was emphasised by two (9, high; 19, high). Respondent 9 explained:

> 'I still wanted to see my dad because I love him and I didn't want to lose him out of my life.' (Respondent 9; aged 13–16)

She was given the opportunity of moving to live with him, but explained:

> 'I was closer to my mum so I stayed with her.' (Respondent 9; aged 13–16)

This meant that she spent

> 'weekends and a few evenings a week with him'. (Respondent 9; aged 13–16)

This was not without its difficulties because parental conflict continued after her parents separated and she was caught in the middle, acting as a 'go-between'.

Similarly, another respondent (19, high) had a strong bond with her father and 'still wanted to see my dad because he's my dad and I love him'. (Respondent 9; aged 13–16)

Parental conflict was evident in her account but subsided when eventually it was arranged that her father would move out of the family home and so she It was arranged that her father would move out of the family home and so she

'saw him at weekends and sometimes in the week'. (Respondent 9; aged 13–16)

The only male respondent (29, medium), to experience parental separation in his teenage years had an extremely negative view of his father, describing him as a 'horrible man'. He explained how before his parents separated:

'Dad was not there much anyway, because of work, so we didn't see much difference for a while.' (Respondent 29; aged 13–16)

He was very candid in describing his reaction to his parents' separation:

'I know I was a bit of a handful as a teenager, I became a bit wild had lots of girlfriends got one of them pregnant and married her. It didn't last long and I've lost contact with my daughter now.' (Respondent 29; aged 13–16)

His siblings were of a similar age and were

'a bit of a nightmare at the time'. (Respondent 29; aged 13–16)

He described his mother's reaction to the separation as one of 'shame' and how, after his father left, his grandmother moved in to support the family.

Stress

Her parents' separation came as shock to one respondent (33, high), who described the stress she felt coping with the changes alongside studying for her GCSE exams, resulting in her becoming unwell (see Chapter Five). The timing of their separation alongside the lack of discussion were key features of her account. Within her family the focus appeared to be on sorting out post-separation arrangements. She felt that

'It was really all about the practicalities, we seemed to avoid talking about feelings, we just sorted out the logistics.' (Respondent 33; aged 13–16)

At the time she

'did not like or want to see my dad after the separation. I also felt loyalty to my mum and was on her side.' (Respondent 33; aged 13–16)

After separation, she continued to live with her mother and brother and considered this an improvement on the previous family situation:

'It didn't make much difference at first really, Dad was away a lot anyway. We all stayed at home apart from him at first. If anything it was less tense and more relaxing.' (Respondent 33; aged 13–16)

'After it all settled down, and Dad had moved out, they eventually started talking properly and things improved.' (Respondent 33; aged 13–16)

It remained unclear whether she renewed contact with her father at a later date.

These teenage respondents had different experiences of parental separation and the changes it brought to their lives, but their accounts show an increasing level of agency which is reflected in the high levels of accommodation recorded by most of the respondents (9, high; 19, high; 33, high) in this age group. In his account Respondent 29 (medium) also showed agency, relieved by his father's absence from the family home, he described his reaction and that of his mother and siblings. He goes on to refer to his earlier marriage and being a parent. His comments elsewhere indicate that his reflections on parental separation are influenced by reflections on his own experience of parenting.

Late teenage years (17–20 years)

Two of the respondents in late teenage years when their parents separated found that this coincided with their entry to higher education and the issues this raised was a dominant theme in their accounts. The remaining respondent (24, lacked continuity) lived at home and experienced parental conflict prior to their separation.

Higher education

Parental separation was a very recent experience for one respondent (12, low) (see case study of Emily in Chapter Five) and the newness and rawness of the experience was evident in her account. The consequences of her parents' decision to separate were beginning to be realised and changes were taking place. Living away from home in a different city at this time hindered communication between Emily and her parents. She found difficulty in concentrating and focusing on her university work and their separation raised questions for her about the quality of her parents' previous relationship and she wondered whether she should return home.

Respondent 34 (lacked continuity) had a similar experience: his parents separated when he moved away from home to attend university in another part of the UK, 12 months earlier.

> 'It happened to me just over a year ago. I am studying in ★★★ and my parents live in Ireland it is difficult to keep in touch with both of them particularly Mum. She was the one to leave and she is not handling it well.' (Respondent 34; aged 17–20)

He recognised that he

> 'sides with Dad'. (Respondent 34; aged 17–20)

Like Respondent 12, his initial reaction affected his

> 'ability to concentrate on work, my job, everything'. (Respondent 34; aged 17–20)

A consequence of his parents' separation had been a change in his living arrangements. While he lived in a house in the city where he was studying during term time, during vacations

'Instead of living with both my mum and dad I am just living with him now.' (Respondent 34; aged 17–20)

He said that his mother was not adjusting as well as she might, although his father appeared happier following the separation. His brother seemed to accept the situation, perhaps helped by seeing a friend go through a similar situation:

'My brother has seen this happen to his friend and he seems OK with it. It happened just over a year ago and Dad seems happier. So maybe it was the best thing.' (Respondent 34; aged 17–20)

Respondent 24 (lacked continuity) lived at home when her parents separated, an event which brought about an end to parental conflict and which she viewed entirely positively. She also described her mother's reaction as one of 'relief'. However, there was a mixed response among her siblings, her older sisters were living independently by this time and she explains how

'Most of us could see what Dad was really like. But my sister – the youngest – still thinks he can't do any wrong.' (Respondent 24; aged 17–20)

The experiences of young adults in this age group were varied, this was reflected in their different levels of accommodation of parental separation and post-separation changes. For those experiencing parental separation as they entered higher education, this was a current issue as their responses showed, and a period of adjustment was needed before they could reflect. Responses elsewhere indicate that while the remaining respondent (24) was very relieved by her father's departure she felt that action could have been taken earlier to improve the family's situation.

Higher levels of accommodation where changes were minimised

In describing their reactions, respondents referred to the changes that took place after their parents separated and their thoughts on these changes. Accounts reflected the diverse nature of children's experiences and family circumstances. As in the PSV, a number found their reactions to the separation and the changes it brought differed from those of their siblings. Where this was the case it could exacerbate their feeling of isolation particularly when, as in Respondent 28's case, it led to them living apart from their siblings. In contrast, where post-separation changes were minimised – children were able to maintain contact with both parents and retain friendship groups within the local area and at school – higher levels of accommodation were seen.

Those in their early years (0–4 years) had difficulty recalling a time when their parents lived together and were unaware of the reason for their parents' separation at the time. Whereas those in middle and late childhood showed greater awareness of their family situation and the changes separation brought, contact with their non-resident parent was a dominant theme in their accounts and those in middle childhood highlighted the time needed to adjust to these changes. Most change was experienced by those in late childhood, many of whom lived with their father and often a step-parent after separation, in some cases moving school to do so, some lost contact with their non-resident parent with little or no explanation. In describing their reaction to the separation, those in their teenage years often had their views about post-separation arrangements taken into account, no doubt exerting some influence on their reactions. Feelings of rawness, shock and disbelief could be seen in the accounts of respondents whose experience of separation coincided with entry to higher education. A very recent event in their lives, their reactions showed some of the issues they faced adjusting to the changed family situation while living away from home.

Across the study many children maintained relationships with both parents after separation, albeit with the inclusion of a step-parent in some cases. Where this took place in the absence of parental conflict, they showed a high level of accommodation irrespective of their age. In these cases, post-separation changes were minimised and children benefited from being able to maintain relationships with both parents, which supported their adjustment. Many continued to attend the same school, providing continuity in friendship groups, which was important in meeting their support needs and aided their adjustment. In this way, children could see that they 'mattered' to their parents and that their needs had been taken into account in decisions about post-separation arrangements (Maes et al, 2011).

There were many reasons why contact was lost, maybe a parent went to live in another country (13, 30) or was imprisoned (20) or because that was what the child wanted (24, 29, 33). Where contact with the non-resident parent ended after separation, there was a greater likelihood of the young adult having a lower level of accommodation of parental separation, most had a medium level (5, 32, 33) or their response lacked continuity (13, 20, 24), occasionally they had a high level because this reflected what they wanted (29).

Discussion

The absence of the non-resident parent from children's lives could be sorely felt (Wade and Smart, 2002; Bagshaw, 2007; Brand et al, 2017) and was particularly significant for boys in late childhood (9–12 years) who showed lower levels of accommodation of post-separation changes as a result (Butler et al, 2003). Loss of contact often led to a sense of divided loyalties, which was exacerbated where children felt unable to talk about their non-resident parent at home (Dunn and Deater-Deckard, 2001). In such circumstances, children's adjustment was affected and they often responded by creating some emotional distance. This was reflected in their medium level of accommodation.

The timing of parental separation exerted considerable impact on children's lives, particularly when it coincided with life transitions such as studying for GCSE exams or leaving home to study at university. The anxiety and stress it caused is shown in respondents' reactions (Flowerdew and Neale, 2003). The 'uniquely uncertain position' of young adults who experienced their parents' divorce as they moved to university was outlined in Abetz and Wang's study (2017); they found that young adults were uncertain about the length of their parents' unhappiness, their new roles, navigating holiday and family events and were concerned about being 'caught in the middle'.

Where a number of changes took place in quick succession children found difficulty accepting them, there were indications that they had insufficient 'psychological travelling time' to make the necessary adjustment (Flowerdew and Neale, 2003), sometimes they felt that their parents prioritised their own needs (Bagshaw, 2007). This was reflected in their lower level of accommodation.

Having examined children's reactions to their parents' separation and post-separation changes in this chapter, we move on to consider the support available to them and the opportunities they had to talk to people about the separation in Chapter Seven (Support).

SEVEN

Support

Case study:
Bethany's story

Bethany (Respondent 23) is 20 years old, she was aged 5–8 years when her parents separated. She was told about the separation by both parents as soon as they decided to separate and describes how:

'Like one of the girls [in the PSV], I used to want to turn the clock back so that we could all be happy again.'

Initially she was

'upset and scared because I was only young, so did not fully understand why they were separating…I saw it in a simple way and pleaded with my mum not to leave Dad.'

Following their separation, she and her 'older sister moved with my mum to a different area of Liverpool'. This involved a lot of changes including

'how often I saw my dad and me and my sister had to adjust to a new school and home'.

She believes that her views and those of her sister were taken into account about post-separation changes:

'but not as much as if my parents separated now, because of our ages'.

Bethany identified her older sister as her sole source of support during these changes:

'Me and my sister stuck together – that made me feel better but as she was the oldest I think she felt responsible for me.'

She felt able to talk to her mother (resident parent) and sister about the separation. When asked whether she would have liked the opportunity to talk to someone outside the family about the separation, she said 'at the time I don't think so', hinting that she may have done at a later date.

Looking back, she says

'I can see now that we were all better for the split in the long run, my mum, dad, sister and me. In fact it might have been better even earlier.'

Bethany had a high level of accommodation.

This chapter examines the support available to children at the time of their parents' separation, the opportunities they had to talk to people about the separation and the extent to which these factors influenced their level of accommodation. It goes on to examine views on whether they would have liked the opportunity to talk about their parents' separation with someone outside the family.

The chapter is in four parts. In the first part, the people providing support for children at the time of their parents' separation are identified; the data is represented in graph form. Respondents seldom commented specifically on the support that they received; where they did, their comments are included. Four main themes emerged regarding the influence support had on respondents' levels of accommodation: the positive impact of parental support, the role of grandmothers, the importance of friends and the isolation of those who identified no one.

The second part of the chapter identifies the people to whom respondents talked about their parents' separation; the data is represented in graph form. Children identified fewer people to whom they talked than those they regarded as sources of support. Any comments made by respondents are included. Three main themes emerged regarding the influence that talking to someone had on respondents' levels of accommodation: the positive impact of being able to talk to parent(s) and siblings, the importance of friends and the negative impact of having no one to talk to.

Drawing on Question 18 which asked respondents whether they would have liked the chance to talk to someone outside the family about what was happening, and if so, who this might be, respondents' views on whether they would have liked this opportunity are reported in the third part of the chapter.

The chapter concludes by examining the extent to which having access to support at the time of separation and the opportunity to talk to people about what was happening, influenced respondent's levels of accommodation of parental separation and post-separation changes.

The chapter started with Bethany's story, one of the respondents in the study. Her account shows that she experienced a number of post-separation changes, including where she lived, the school she attended and how often she saw her father. Throughout these changes she felt supported by her older sister and was able to talk to her about the separation; her comments show that they had a strong bond She also felt able to talk to her mother about the separation but interestingly did not see her as a source of support. She found this level of support sufficient and at the time would not have wanted the opportunity to talk to someone outside the family about her parents' separation. She had a high level of accommodation.

Support

Respondents' accounts were analysed for their views and experience of support during parental separation and post-separation changes. There was a particular focus on Question 13, which asked who their main source of support was during the changes and provided the following options for their response: mother; father; brother(s); sister(s); grandmother; grandfather; aunt; uncle; cousin(s); friend(s); no one and other, with an open text box to identify who this was. It was up to respondents to interpret 'support' in their own way.

The people identified as providing support during their parents' separation are shown in Figure 7.1. Respondents most often identified their mothers [21], grandmothers [15] and fathers [12]. Many felt supported by members of their extended family, in particular aunts [10], grandfathers [6], uncles [5] and cousins [3]. Siblings were less often seen as providing support [4]. A few identified sources of support outside the family such as friends [5] and a youth club leader (Respondent 29). Seven respondents said that no one provided support for them during the changes. [Note: Numbers in square brackets refer to the total number of respondents in each category.]

Within the family

Parent(s)

The majority of respondents [22] identified at least one parent as providing support during post-separation changes; 21 identified their

Figure 7.1: Respondents' sources of support during post-separation changes

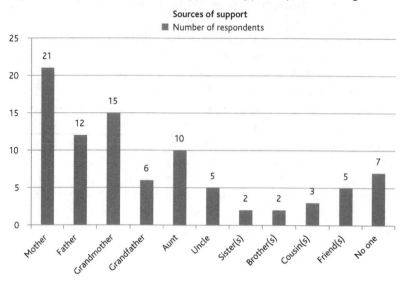

Sources of support
■ Number of respondents

mother, 12 their father, of whom 11 identified both parents. Where mothers were identified, they were always the resident parent. Notably, fathers were not identified as the only source of parental support unless they were the resident parent.

Most respondents who were supported by both parents had a high level of accommodation of parental separation. This was the case for seven (6, 8, 9, 14, 18, 19, 26) of the 11 respondents. However, where children's experiences were affected by parental conflict (1, 17) or when parental separation was a recent event (12) despite feeling supported by both parents, a low level of accommodation was recorded.

Grandparent(s)

Grandparents were seen as an important source of support by many respondents. Grandmothers were particularly important and were identified by 15 respondents (3, 5, 6, 7, 8, 10, 12, 13, 14, 18, 21, 22, 25, 26, 30), grandfathers by six (3, 5, 10, 13, 14, 21). Grandfathers always featured alongside grandmothers.

In most cases, grandparent(s) were identified alongside parent(s), meaning that these respondents had access to a range of support at the time of separation. Where this was the case, higher levels of accommodation were recorded, with eight (6, 8, 10, 14, 18, 21, 25, 26) out of the 12 respondents saying that they were supported by their grandparents and at least one parent. The remaining respondents referred to loss of contact with their father after separation (5) or recency of the event (12).

Where grandmothers were a child's only source of support (7, 22, 30) they played a vital role in their lives, often taking on the role of resident parent. In these cases, respondents were in their early years (0–4 years) when their parents separated and could not remember much about when their parents lived together.

Following her parents' separation, Respondent 30 (high) moved with her father to live with her grandparents. Her mother moved to Egypt, leading to very limited contact; as a consequence her grandmother became a very significant person in her life:

> 'Nan has been like a mum to me.' (Respondent 30; aged 0–4)

In her account, Respondent 22 (Gemma, case study in Chapter Six) described the many changes that took place in her family after separation and the important role that her grandmother played in her life, particularly when she reached secondary school age and went to live with her.

Respondent 7 found that her grandmother was someone who could be relied upon for support when, after her parents separated, she lived with her mother and

> 'Mum's new partner who got drunk and caused trouble when he came home late'. (Respondent 7; aged 0–4)

The importance of grandmothers in supporting these respondents was evident from their accounts.

Extended family

Aunts often played a role in children's lives (see Respondent 9's account in Chapter Nine) and were usually seen as a source of support alongside grandmothers and at least one parent. Respondents (3, 8, 10, 14, 21, 25, 26) who had access to such a network of support during their parents' separation had a high level of accommodation of post-separation changes.

One respondent (32) identified his aunt as his only source of support. He did not explain how his aunt supported him, but did express his 'frustration and anger' at all the changes that took place at that time. He had a medium level of accommodation.

Uncles (3, 8, 14, 25, 26) and cousins (3, 14, 25) were sometimes identified and always featured alongside aunts. In this way they formed part of a larger support network involving at least one parent and often a grandmother.

Siblings

Four respondents identified their siblings as providing support, two (23, 29) identified their sister(s) and two (6, 18) their brother(s). Where siblings were identified, they usually featured in the context of a wider support network including at least one parent (29), and sometimes their grandmother (6, 18). These respondents showed a high level of accommodation.

In Bethany's (23) situation (described in the case study at the beginning of this chapter), her sister was her only source of support. She described how they 'stuck together' which made her 'feel better' but recognised the responsibility that her sister might have felt as the older sibling.

Outside the family

Friends

Friends were a source of support for some respondents, particularly among those in late childhood (8, 13, 26) or teenage years (9, 19) at the time of separation. One (9) explained their importance in her life:

> 'Friends were really important to me and I didn't want to leave them...I was given the chance to see a counsellor but didn't want to. I had a good support network of friends and youth group that helped me through.' (Respondent 9; aged 13–16)

Alongside their friends, these respondents had access to a wide range of support including at least one parent and their grandmother or their aunt. This was reflected in most (8, 9, 19, 26) showing a high level of accommodation.

Professionals

Only one respondent (29) identified a professional source of support: his youth club leader. He also had support from his mother and sister(s).

A more detailed account of his experience can be found in the section on 'professionals' below.

No one

Seven respondents (2, 4, 11, 15, 16, 31, 33) said that no one supported them during the separation and appeared isolated. Most were in middle or late childhood at the time of their parents' separation. They gave diverse accounts of their experiences, reference to parental conflict being a feature in three accounts (2, 11, 31). Levels of accommodation varied across the group, five showing a high level (4, 11, 15, 16, 31), one a medium level (33) and one a low level (2).

People to whom respondents talked

Respondents' accounts were analysed to establish whom they talked to about their parents' separation. There was a particular focus on Question 17, which asked who they felt able to talk to about their parents' separation. The following options were provided: mother; father; brother(s); sister(s); grandmother; grandfather; aunt; uncle; teacher; youth worker; social worker; counsellor; friend(s) and other with an open text box to identify who this was. Analysis of open text box responses elsewhere provided additional information in a few cases.

The people respondents talked to about their parents' separation are shown in Figure 7.2. Within the family, respondents most often identified their mothers [12] as people to whom they talked. They also talked to fathers [7] and grandmothers [7] as well as grandfathers [4], aunts [3] and uncles [2]. Many talked to their siblings [9] who were viewed as confidants rather than sources of support.

There was some overlap between those people whom respondents identified as sources of support and those to whom they felt able to talk. Overall, they identified fewer people they talked to about the separation than sources of support.

Outside the family, many respondents talked to friends [11], some talked to professionals, such as youth workers [3], counsellors [3] or social workers [2]. None reported talking to teachers. Eight respondents said that they talked to no one about the separation.

Figure 7.2: People to whom respondents talked about their parents' separation

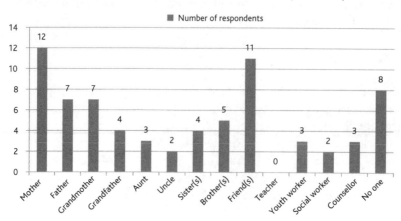

Within the family

Parent(s)

Children were most likely to talk about the separation with their parents, most often their mothers [12] but sometimes their fathers [7]. Five (6, 8, 18, 26, 34) were able to talk to both parents. With the exception of one (34), they also identified both parents as sources of support, indicating that they were well supported and able to talk openly about the separation and changes it brought, this was reflected in a high level of accommodation. (For respondent 34, parental separation was a recent event which occurred as he moved to university.)

The remaining seven respondents (10, 13, 21, 23, 24, 25, 27) talked to their mother and two (3, 14) to their father. In these cases their father was their resident parent, most also identified this parent as a source of support (Respondent 23 being the exception). Most of these respondents showed a high level of accommodation (3, 10, 14, 21, 25, 27) but two lacked continuity (13, 24).

Overall, respondents were less likely to identify parent(s) as people to whom they could talk about the separation than as sources of support. This pattern was evident across all levels of accommodation and ages.

Grandparent(s)

After parents, children were most likely to talk to their grandparents about the separation: seven (3, 8, 10, 14, 21, 26, 30) spoke to their grandmothers, four of whom (3, 10, 14, 21) also talked to their grandfather, in each case these people were identified as sources of support. Being able to talk to their grandmother appeared to hold particular importance for those aged 9–12 or 0–4 at the time of their parents' separation.

Respondents who identified their grandmother as someone they talked to about the separation were also able to talk to at least one of their parents (Respondent 30 was an exception), meaning that they had the opportunity to talk about the separation and ask questions about the changes it would bring. They were well supported in adjusting to their parents' separation and the changes it brought. The positive impact of this could be seen in their high level of accommodation.

Extended family

A few respondents talked to members of the extended family: three spoke to their aunts (8, 25, 26) and two to their uncles (8, 26), and they were also identified as sources of support. These respondents had high levels of accommodation.

Siblings

Nine respondents identified their siblings as people they talked to about the separation: four (3, 14, 23, 31) talked to their sister(s) and five (6, 8, 11, 18, 26), to their brother(s). Children were more likely to view siblings as someone to whom they could talk rather than as a source of support; nonetheless siblings were never the only person to whom they talked, most had been able to speak to one or both of their parents, or sometimes friends. These respondents were well supported and showed a high level of accommodation.

Outside the family

Friends

Eleven respondents (1, 8, 9, 11, 12, 17, 18, 25, 26, 31, 34) talked to friends about the separation. Being able to talk to friends was important across the whole age range, although half (1, 8, 11, 17, 26, 31) were aged 9–12 at the time of separation suggesting that friends were particularly important to this age group.

Most were also able to talk to family members including parents and siblings (8, 11, 18, 25, 26, 31, 34) and, with the exception of 34 (for whom parental separation was a recent event), all had a high level of accommodation. Two (9, 12) indicated that they had relied upon talking to friends, identifying no one else to whom they were able to talk; one (9) had a high level of accommodation while the other (12) had a low level, attributable to the separation having occurred recently. As well as talking to friends, two (1, 17) spoke to social workers (see the next section on Professionals).

Professionals

Eight respondents (1, 7, 8, 17, 22, 26, 29, 34) talked to professionals about their parents' separation; some talked to counsellors (7, 22, 34), others to youth workers (8, 26, 29) and to social workers (1, 17). They did not say when these discussions took place, who arranged them or whether they had any choice about talking to them, the exception being respondent 34, who on experiencing his parents' separation after he moved to university, explained how he had sought counselling for himself because:

> 'I was finding everything really difficult and so I went to counselling which really helped. Also my girl friend has been very supportive and tries to help me. My friends that I live with also have been there.' (Respondent 34; aged 17–20)

As an adult he made his own decisions about what kind of advice he wanted, when he sought it and from whom he sought it. It is evident from his account that he found the counselling which he received beneficial, but it was not possible to assess his level of accommodation because his account lacked continuity.

The other respondents (7, 22) who talked to counsellors were very young (aged 0–4) at the time of separation and faced additional issues as a result of post-separation arrangements. Respondent 7 referred to her mother's new partner, with whom they lived, getting drunk and causing trouble when he came home late. The only person she talked to about the separation was the counsellor, as a young adult she had a high level of accommodation. Gemma's (22) story is told at the beginning of Chapter Six, her account showed a medium level of accommodation. In each case it was unclear who arranged the counselling sessions, their age when they took place and their views on their effectiveness.

Those respondents (8, 26) who talked to youth workers about their parents' separation were in late childhood (aged 9–12) at the time of separation. They were able to talk to many people, including both parents about the separation and had access to support from their extended family, they had a high level of accommodation.

The remaining respondent (29) was in his teenage years at the time; he talked to his youth club leader as well as his work supervisor about his parents' separation. He did not comment on the value of these conversations, but it is evident that he faced particular challenges at that time. He explained how his grandmother moved to live with the family after his father left and described his intense dislike of his father. He could not remember how he felt when his parents separated because he

'probably chose not to'. (Respondent 29; aged 13–16)

His youth club leader was a source of support alongside his mother and sisters. His account showed a high level of accommodation.

Respondents (1, 17) who spoke to social workers did so as part of Family Court proceedings to establish their views in relation to residence and contact arrangements because their parents were unable to reach agreement. Given their age at the time (9–12 years) their views would have informed rather than determined the arrangements made by the court. They did not refer to the experience of talking to a social worker about their parents' separation and post-separation arrangements. A high level of on-going parental conflict was evident in their accounts which are described in more detail in Chapter Nine. They showed a low level of accommodation.

No one

Nine respondents (2, 4, 5, 7, 15, 16, 22, 28, 33) spoke to no one about their parents' separation, five of whom (2, 4, 15, 16, 33) identified no one as a source of support, meaning that they were particularly isolated. Some described their reaction at the time, explaining how:

'I bottle it up.' (Respondent 2; aged 9–12)

'I never talked much as a kid and kept things to myself.' (Respondent 16; aged 5–8)

'I didn't really talk about it.' (Respondent 33; aged 13–16)

One respondent (28) aged 23, explained how she had never spoken about her parents' separation before completing the questionnaire.

'Nobody, I am a quiet person and keep things to myself. I have never spoken about it before.' (Respondent 28; aged 9–12)

Parental conflict was a feature of her account and offered a possible explanation for her response. A more detailed account of her situation can be found in Chapter Nine.

Views on the opportunity to talk to someone outside the family

When asked whether they would have liked the chance to talk to someone outside the family about their parents' separation at the time, and if so, who that would have been (Question 18), attitudes varied. Some respondents said that they would and identified who might have taken on the role, others said that they would, but did not specify who this might be and others said that they would not.

Those who would have liked the opportunity

Ten respondents would have liked the opportunity to talk to someone, this included half of those (4, 15, 16, 22) who said that they did not have anyone to talk to. Three (2, 16, 24) suggested a teacher or someone in school might have taken on the role, one (16), who experienced parental separation for a second time when her grandparents separated, suggested speaking to

'maybe a teacher in school because I was a bit confused at the time and it would have helped me see it wasn't my fault'. (Respondent 16; aged 5–8)

Parental conflict featured in the lives of two respondents (2, 24) who thought that talking to someone in school would have been beneficial. Experiencing parental separation for a second time, one said:

'I felt very different to the other kids in school and awkward when they asked why I lived with my grandparents. It would have been good if I could have talked to someone in school in confidence to help me.' (Respondent 2; aged 9–12)

Respondent 24's parents separated when she was in her late teenage years. She thought that the involvement of someone in school might have improved her situation sooner:

'Yes. Someone official who could intervene, maybe at school.' (Respondent 24; aged 17–20)

The need for conversations to be in confidence was emphasised by respondents (1, 17) who continued to experience parental conflict in their families. They spoke to social workers, but would have liked the opportunity to talk to a youth worker, or a counsellor:

'Yes, a youth worker or counsellor, as long as it was in confidence,' (Respondent 1; aged 9–12)

'I think we [would] all have been better if we had seen some sort of youth worker who would have helped us not to bottle things up and get us to talk, that would have been better especially if my brothers would have spoken up more.' (Respondent 17; aged 9–12)

While others would have liked the opportunity to talk to someone, their focus was on the reason why rather than who might take on this role:

'I would of, because of lots of things. Dad was thousands of miles away, didn't keep in touch, and Mum struggled for money.' (Respondent 13; aged 9–12)

'It might have helped, it was a bit lonely at home sometimes.' (Respondent 5; aged 9–12)

Moving away to study at university at the same time as her parents separated led one respondent (12) to believe that speaking to a counsellor might be beneficial:

'I may think of going to see a counsellor if I don't feel any better after Christmas.' (Respondent 12; aged 17–20)

Gemma (22) (case study in Chapter Six), thought that it would have been useful to speak to someone, but did not specify who might take on the role:

'It would have been good to have ongoing help and support. I was going through a lot. But it has made me the person I am today.' (Respondent 22; aged 0–4)

Support network sufficient

Some respondents (9, 18, 27) thought that their support network of friends, or family, was sufficient and therefore that they did not need this opportunity:

'I was given the chance to see a counsellor but didn't want to. I had a good support network of friends and youth group that helped me through.' (Respondent 9; aged 13–16)

'I didn't need a counsellor because my friends were really good.' (Respondent 18; aged 0–4)

'Possibly, but Mum has always been there to talk to.' (Respondent 27; aged 0–4)

Sometimes age appeared to be a factor, with one respondent (25), aged 5–8 years at the time of separation, indicating that he would not have liked talking about it then, but hinting that he may have done at a later date:

'I was not ready for that, I was too young and didn't know how to talk about things.' (Respondent 25; aged 5–8)

Those who would not have wanted the opportunity to talk to someone outside the family

Eight respondents (3, 10, 11, 14, 21, 29, 31, 32) would not have wanted the opportunity to talk to someone outside the family. All except one (32), had been able to talk to more than one person about the separation, including at least one parent in half the cases. They found this sufficient and had a high level of accommodation. Respondent 32 had a medium level.

Higher levels of accommodation for those supported by parents

Common patterns emerged from respondents' accounts, with those showing a high level of accommodation of post-separation changes usually identifying parent(s) as a source of support, often alongside their grandmother and sometimes their aunt. Some had been able to talk to their parent(s) about the separation, meaning that they had access to an extensive supportive network within the family. Those in late childhood or teenage years often also identified friends as sources of support. In these cases, children were well supported in adjusting to parental separation and post-separation changes. This was reflected in their level of accommodation.

Fewer sources of support were identified by respondents showing a medium level of accommodation; only three were able to identify family members who supported them, these were their resident parent (5, 28), grandparents (5) and an aunt (32). None of these respondents were able to identify anyone outside the family who supported them, or anyone they could talk to about their parents' separation. Two (16, 33) appeared particularly isolated, being unable to identify either anyone who supported them or to whom they could talk. They indicated that they would have liked the opportunity to talk to someone about the separation at the time, only one (16) indicated who might take on this role.

Respondents who showed a low level of accommodation often identified both parents as sources of support, but their situations were complicated either by on-going conflict despite their parents separating some time ago (1, 17) or by the recent nature of the event and rawness of the experience (12). Most were able to talk to their friends about the separation, but had no opportunity to speak to anyone in the family. Two (1, 17) spoke to social workers as part of Family Court proceedings. These conversations would have focused on their views on residence and contact arrangements with a view to their wishes and feelings being made known to the court rather than on-going support. The opportunity to talk to someone outside the family about their parents' separation, maybe a youth worker or a counsellor, was a common theme in this level.

Discussion

During their parents' separation and post-separation changes, most respondents drew on support from their family, particularly their parent(s), grandparent(s) or extended family members, which assisted children in coping with separation (Du Plooy and Van Rensburg, 2015; Brand et al, 2017; Morrison et al, 2017). Resident parents, usually mothers, held a particular importance, as did grandmothers and their support strongly influenced respondents' levels of accommodation (Dunn and Deater-Deckard, 2001; Butler et al, 2003; Fortin et al, 2012; Brand et al, 2017). Some respondents had access to a large supportive network of extended family members, including parent(s), grandparent(s) as well as aunt(s), uncle(s) and cousins, whereas others identified just one source of support within the family. The number of sources did not influence their level of accommodation, what was significant was that children had access to at least one source of support within the family, which included their resident parent.

Most respondents were able to talk to someone about their parents' separation. Most commonly this was someone within the family, usually their mother or grandmother. Siblings were sometimes identified as people to whom respondents could talk, but they were more likely to be viewed as confidants rather than as sources of support (Butler et al, 2003). Bethany's case shows how sibling order influenced relationships, with older siblings taking on responsibility for younger siblings and younger siblings looking to them as role models (Roth et al, 2014). In cases where family members were identified as sources of support, children were seen to have the advantage of a large network of support on which to draw during the changes that took place.

Outside the family, friends were an important source of support, particularly for children in late childhood and those in their teenage years; many respondents reported being able to talk to friends about their parents' separation and it was evident that they held particular significance for children of all ages (Dunn and Deater-Deckard, 2001; Butler et al, 2003; Du Plooy and Van Rensburg, 2015). Friends, particularly those who have similar experiences, assisted in guiding expectations and in normalising the separation experience (Morrison et al, 2017, 50).

Some children spoke to professionals such as youth workers, counsellors or social workers. In the case of counsellors and youth workers it was not always clear whether respondents exercised choice in this or how they viewed their intervention. Those who spoke to social workers did so in the context of a highly conflicted family situation where their parents were unable to make post-separation arrangements for them, preoccupied with their own concerns, their parents gave little thought to the impact of their behaviour on their children, who experienced 'diminished parenting' as a result (Fortin et al, 2012). One respondent (1) who talked to a social worker highlighted the need for discussions to be 'in confidence' maybe giving an indication of her view on this experience. An interesting consideration of children's views on involvement in 'parenting coordination' in Canada can be found in Quigley and Cyr's work (2018). They found that most children thought it important for their voice to be heard because it helped the Parenting Coordinator understand their needs and the issues within their family and that the decisions made affected the whole family. Meetings with the Coordinator provided 'a safe place to open up about their feelings' and involvement in parenting coordination gave children a better understanding of what was happening and allowed them to stay informed (Quigley and Cyr, 2018, 510).

Some respondents said that they had not been able to talk to anyone about their parents' separation, and where this coincided with their inability to identify a source of support, respondents appeared particularly isolated. With fewer sources of support and no one to talk to about their parents' separation, many of these children had to navigate the changes which parental separation brought, including the loss of contact with their father in some cases (5, 32, 33), with no support. Adjusting to post-separation changes without the benefit of family support or support from anyone outside the family gave rise to questions about the extent to which these respondents felt that they 'mattered' in their parents' (or grandparents') separation and was reflected in their lower level of accommodation (Moxnes, 2003; Maes et al, 2011). Some indicated that they would have liked the opportunity to talk to someone about their parents' separation, maybe a teacher or a counsellor (2, 16, 24).

This chapter examined the support available to children at the time of parental separation and the opportunities they had to talk to people about the separation. Children who felt supported by their parent(s) and were able to talk to them about the separation and changes that were taking place were found to have a higher level of accommodation of parental separation as young adults. The next chapter focuses on the quality of parental communication at the time of separation and post-separation changes. In doing so it builds on the knowledge gained in this chapter and highlights the importance of good communication between parent(s) and their child and its influence on accommodation of parental separation over time.

EIGHT

Communication

Case study:
Joseph's story

Joseph (Respondent 5) is 18 years old, he was aged 9–12 when his parents separated. Having viewed the PSV he thought that it was realistic and said that it showed some of how he felt when his parents separated. He found out that they were separating at the time of his father leaving and was told what was happening by his mother.

After separation he lived with his mother and sisters. Apart from no longer living with his father there was no change in his living arrangements or the school he attended.

When asked whether his views were taken into account about any changes, he replied:

'It wasn't up to me.'

After separation he lost contact with his father. He described his thoughts and feelings at the time:

'It was hard not seeing Dad or hearing from him.'

He felt supported by his mother, grandmother and grandfather, but identified no one to whom he could talk. He explained:

'Mum and my sisters were always having a go about Dad and I didn't feel I could mention his name at home.'

He would have liked the opportunity to talk to someone outside the family about what was happening, he was unsure who that might be but thought that:

'It might have helped, it was a bit lonely at home sometimes.'

Asked how he feels about the changes now, he says simply:

'I've moved on.'

Joseph had a medium level of accommodation.

This chapter focuses on communication, specifically the quality of communication that parents had with their children during separation, and when making post-separation arrangements. Respondents' accounts showed that this varied widely, with some children given explanations about what was happening and feeling included in decisions about post-separation arrangements and others receiving little or no explanation, and having to make sense of the situation themselves. The opportunity to maintain contact with their non-resident parent was a key aspect of the quality of parental communication which children experienced.

To understand children's experience of parental communication, their accounts were examined to establish when respondents learned about their parents' separation and who told them (Question 7), and when post-separation changes happened, whether their views were taken into account and if so, in what way (Question 12). Accounts were also scrutinised for any evidence of contact with their non-resident parent after separation. These factors allowed the quality of parental communication with their children at the time of separation and after separation to be assessed and its impact on respondents' levels of accommodation to be determined.

The chapter focuses on three particular areas of children's experience: learning about the separation in advance, having their views taken into account in post-separation changes and not having their views taken into account. The availability of parental support and opportunity to talk to parents about the separation are recognised as being part of parental communication, therefore this chapter should be read alongside Chapter Seven (Support).

The chapter started with Joseph's story (5), who describes his experience of limited communication with one parent (mother) and no communication with the other (father) after separation, and how it affected his life. As a boy in late childhood he found the loss of contact with his father difficult, a situation exacerbated by feeling unable to mention his name at home. Over time he created emotional distance from these events, and as a young adult showed a medium level of accommodation.

The positive impact of good parental communication was emphasised in respondents' accounts and three consistent findings emerged. Children were seen to benefit from: parent(s) informing them of their separation in advance, this provided some explanation and gave them time to think about the changes that might take place; feeling their views had been taken into account in post-separation changes, even if they had not been asked about them directly and being able to maintain contact with their non-resident parent.

Learning about the separation in advance

Respondents were asked when they were told that their parents were going to separate and who told them. They were able to select their response from the following options: as soon as my parents decided to separate; a few weeks before one parent left; at the time of one parent leaving; found out by overhearing parents arguing (these accounts are considered in Chapter Nine); found out after one parent left. They were able to identify the person who told them in an open text box (Question 7).

Many children learned about their parents' separation in advance: eleven (6, 8, 9, 18, 19, 20, 23, 24, 26, 28, 33) were told as soon as their parents decided to separate and three (10, 12, 21) a few weeks before one parent left. Most respondents who identified the person who told them said that it was their mother (9, 10, 12, 19, 21, 24, 33), who then became their resident parent after separation, but some (6, 18, 23) had been told by both parents. These children had advance notice of forthcoming changes in their family and therefore were in a position to think about, consider and ask questions about the changes that might take place.

As Chapter Five (Emotions) showed, age played a significant part in children's initial responses, with those in the youngest age group (0-4 years) reporting being too young to understand what was happening (6, 18) and those in middle and late childhood showing that they had some understanding of what was happening, albeit this may have been limited.

For example, Respondent 23 felt:

> 'upset and scared because I was only young, so did not fully understand why they were separating', (Respondent 23; aged 5–8)

She went on to explain that she saw the situation:

'in a simple way and pleaded with my mum not to leave Dad'. (Respondent 23; aged 5–8)

As they reached teenage years, respondents brought a greater level of understanding and sometimes experience to the news. Some anticipated the event because their parents had separated previously and then reconciled (9, 19). While they recognised that their parents' separation was a possibility, on realising that their separation was permanent this time, they could be upset:

> 'I knew it was coming so I wasn't surprised. They'd separated twice before so I kind of knew what to expect. I was still upset though because I thought, "This time it's actually happening and they're never getting back together again."' (Respondent 9; aged 13–16)

For others it came as a shock, as in Respondent 33's case, who described her initial reaction when her parents separated while she was studying for her GCSE exams:

> 'My first response was devastation – I couldn't believe it was happening.' (Respondent 33; aged 13–16)

Where parental conflict was a feature of their parents' relationship and separation brought it to an end, respondents' (10, 24, 28) relief was palpable, whatever their age.

Learning at the time of one parent leaving or afterwards

Just under a quarter of respondents (eight) (3, 5, 13, 14, 16, 25, 32, 34) learned of their parents' separation at the time of one parent leaving. Most were told by their mother (3, 5, 13, 14, 34), occasionally by their father (32). The confusion this created was apparent in many accounts. A lack of knowledge meant that they were unable to prepare for the event and their immediate response was often combined with feelings of anger and upset:

> 'I didn't know why this had happened and I was confused and annoyed with my parents for letting it happen.' (Respondent 32; aged 9–12)

Some respondents were unaware that their parents had separated until a parent had left the family home. With no explanation of what had happened, those in middle childhood (4, 15) tended to blame themselves:

> 'I was very upset and a bit angry and I think I felt that my siblings and I had done something to cause all this.' (Respondent 4; aged 5–8)

> 'I thought it was my fault. I tried to pretend it wasn't happening by not thinking about it.' (Respondent 15; aged 5–8)

One (25) saw her father leaving without explanation, which provoked a strong emotional response:

> 'I hated my mum for making my dad leave.' (Respondent 25; aged 5–8)

Five respondents (1, 2, 11, 17, 31) learned of their parents' separation by overhearing their parents arguing; their accounts are considered in Chapter Nine.

Whether views were taken into account

Determining whether respondent's views were taken into consideration when post-separation changes were put into place relied on analysis of responses to Question 12 alongside reported changes in living arrangements, school attended and adults with whom they lived (Question 10). Accounts were scrutinised for reference to contact with their non-resident parent after separation.

Responses were then grouped according to whether respondents said that their views had been taken into account, had not been taken into account or had been taken into account by a social worker. It should be noted that eight respondents (2, 6, 7, 8, 18, 26, 27, 33) did not answer this question.

Where views were taken into account

Twelve respondents (3, 9, 10, 11, 14, 19, 21, 23, 25, 28, 31, 33) said that their views were taken into account by their parent(s) when determining post-separation arrangements. Some (3, 14, 28) had direct discussions with parents about with whom they wanted to live:

'We were asked who we wanted to live with.' (Respondent 3; aged 9–12)

'They did ask me about where I wanted to live.' (Respondent 28; aged 9–12)

Some also had discussions about contact arrangements and school:

'I was allowed to say if I did or didn't want to go to Dad's. I was involved with discussions about where to go to school.' (Respondent 25; aged 5–8)

One (23) said that while her views had been taken into account, they would have had greater weight if she had been older:

'Yes, but not as much as they would've if my parents would of separated now, because of our ages now.' (Respondent 23; aged 5–8)

Others were not asked specifically about their views, but believed that they had been taken into account because of the decisions which their parents made:

'Yes, because my mum was keen for us to keep in touch with our school and friends.' (Respondent 31; aged 9–12)

'I didn't want to move house because I had friends who were really important to me and I didn't want to leave them, so we stayed in the same house until Mum remarried, then we moved but I wasn't happy. Dad still lives in the village though, so I still get to see all my friends.' (Respondent 9; aged 13–16)

'A bit, about school and where we were going to live.' (Respondent 11; aged 9–12)

'It was OK until we moved to a different home a few years later. Then I missed my friends and familiar places. Up until then it was OK.' (Respondent 19; aged 13–16)

Two respondents (10, 21) who referred to domestic violence thought that their mother's decision to leave their father was based on their fear in the family home, meaning that their views had been taken into account. Their accounts are considered in more detail in Chapter Nine.

> 'My mum knew I was getting scared and this made her leave Dad I think.' (Respondent 21; aged 9–12)

> 'Yes, I believe it was my fear that finally made my mum leave Dad and so I suppose my feelings were taken into account.' (Respondent 10; aged 9–12)

Interestingly, in almost a reversal of roles, one respondent (34) at university when his parents separated, referred to his parents asking for his views almost in an advisory way:

> 'Well, Mum listened to what I said but has not acted on it. Dad has taken my views and has asked me what should he do and I have tried to give the best answers I can.' (Respondent 34; aged 17–20)

Scrutiny of these accounts indicated that most respondents maintained contact with their non-resident parent after separation, one (33) did not and the position of three (11, 28, 31) was unknown.

These respondents felt able to influence the decisions made about post-separation arrangements, either directly by being asked for their views, or indirectly by their parents taking account of their situation in the decisions that they made. The beneficial effect of such communication was reflected in the high level of accommodation of parental separation recorded across most of the group, those who lost contact with their non-resident parent (33) or daily contact with their siblings (28) being exceptions.

Where views were not taken into account

Eight respondents (4, 5, 12, 13, 15, 22, 29, 32) said that their views were not taken into account in post-separation changes. Some (5, 13) felt that they should not have been and that it was their parents who should decide the arrangements (see the case study of Joseph at the beginning of the chapter). Sadly, they lost contact with their father after separation which they experienced as a significant loss and was reflected in their levels of accommodation. Respondent 5 had a medium level and Respondent 13 lacked continuity.

The frustration felt by older children when their parents' separation brought many changes, including loss of contact with a parent and their views were not taken into account, were clearly evident in some cases:

> 'frustration and anger at changes happening. We moved to another area and it messed up school and friends...I didn't like what was happening nor did my brother but he accepted that we had a step-father living with us.' (Respondent 32; aged 9–12)

He showed a medium level of accommodation.

Some respondents' views (4, 29) were not taken into account and they lost contact with their father after separation, however where this was what they wanted at the time, it was reflected in high levels of accommodation. After separation, Respondent 4 lived with her mother and grandparents, and she lost contact with her father for a while as she explained:

> 'didn't see Dad. I didn't want to for a long while.' (Respondent 4; aged 5–8)

Following his parents' separation his grandmother moved to live with Respondent 29, his mother and his siblings. He saw the lack of contact as beneficial because

> 'My dad was a horrible man and it was great for us all to be rid of him to be honest.' (Respondent 29; aged 13–16)

Sometimes respondents were of the opinion that their views were not sought because they were seen as 'too young' by their parents such as Respondent 22, Gemma (see case study in Chapter Six) who said:

> 'It was never discussed and I was not asked what I thought. I think they thought I was too young.' (Respondent 22; aged 0–4)

Parental separation was a very recent event for one respondent (12) who was still trying to understand what had happened to bring about the end of her parents' relationship, post-separation arrangements remained a 'work in progress' and she had a low level of accommodation reflecting her on-going adjustment to these changes.

The variation in levels of accommodation across this group suggest that where respondents did not have their views taken into account in post-separation arrangements they were more likely to exhibit a lower level accommodation.

Views were taken into account by a social worker

The accounts of two respondents (1, 17) showed a high level of parental conflict; they learned of their parents' separation by overhearing them arguing and their parents were unable to reach agreement on post-separation arrangements, turning to the Family Courts to resolve the matter. This led to the two children meeting with a social worker to talk about their views on post-separation arrangements, namely residence and contact:

'Dad said he was going to court to "keep us" and we saw a social worker.' (Respondent 1; aged 9–12)

'because Dad and Mum could not agree a social worker and the courts had to sort it all out and we spoke to a social worker'. (Respondent 17; aged 9–12)

They made no comment on the experience of talking to a social worker in their accounts but a high level of parental conflict continued to be a feature within their families, bringing about a low level of accommodation. Their experiences are discussed in more detail in Chapter Nine.

Higher levels of accommodation for those who had good communication

The quality of parental communication during parental separation and through post-separation changes differed significantly across the levels of accommodation. Some children learned of their parents' separation in advance, being told as soon as their parents decided to separate or a few weeks before one parent left, these children had advance notice of future changes in their family. When linked with their view that their needs had been taken into account in post-separation changes and the opportunity to maintain contact with both parents, these children (9,

10, 19, 23,) were seen to experience good parental communication, the benefits of which could be seen in their high level of accommodation.

This benefit disappeared when children learned of their parents' separation in advance and had their views about post-separation changes taken into account, but lost contact with their non-resident parent (33) or siblings (28). This was reflected in their medium level of accommodation.

Some children found out about the separation at the time of a parent leaving or after they had left; in these cases their parents' separation came as an unpleasant surprise leading to confusion, a lack of understanding and a range of emotions. Their parents' actions failed to give any notice of forthcoming changes, leaving children unprepared, which contributed to their sense of confusion. Where subsequently parents went on to take account of their child's views in the changes that took place, ensuring that contact with their non-resident parent was maintained, children (11, 14, 21, 25, 31) had a high level of accommodation, showing how initial difficulties could be ameliorated by improved communication between parents and a sensitive response to their needs.

The way in which respondents felt that their views were taken into account about post-separation changes differed across the group: some (10, 21) saw their parents' separation as a response to their needs, particularly where they expressed fear as a result of domestic violence; others (9, 11, 31) saw their parents' commitment to providing continuity in arrangements, such as where they lived and went to school as indications that their views had been taken into consideration. The positive effect of children believing that their views had been taken into account in the decision-making was reflected in their high level of accommodation.

Children's exclusion from decision-making could lead to confusion, distress and sadness, older children who experienced many changes (32) with little or no regard for their views could feel angry and frustrated by them. Where children felt excluded and that their needs had not been taken into account in post-separation arrangements, particularly where they lost contact with their non-resident parent, they felt they did not 'matter' to their parents, they created emotional distance over time and this was reflected in medium levels of accommodation (5, 22, 32).

Being provided with an explanation, having their views taken into account about post-separation changes and being able to maintain contact with their non-resident parent provided evidence of good communication between parents and their child and were key factors in bringing about a higher level of accommodation.

Discussion

Where, one or both parent(s), advised children of the separation and provided an explanation as well as the opportunity to ask questions about events, children were able to create 'meaning' and develop some understanding about the changes taking place. Such communication enabled children to deal with their feelings and anxieties about the future more easily and helped guide their expectations (Butler et al, 2002; Morrison et al, 2017). This was associated with a higher level of accommodation and supports findings in earlier studies (Maes et al, 2011; Morrison et al, 2017).

In contrast, the 'sudden and unexplained absence of a parent' often led to considerable distress, confusion and sadness and contributed to unhappiness with post-separation arrangements (Hogan et al, 2003, 169). It created difficulties for children in accepting the changed situation and was reflected in lower levels of accommodation.

Children saw their views taken into consideration in a number of different ways, however not all saw themselves as having a role in the decision-making process, taking the view that this was their parents' responsibility (5, 13). Children might see the actions of their parents in choosing to separate (10, 21) or ensuring continuity in where they lived and the school they attended (11, 31) as indications that their views were taken into consideration and that they 'mattered' in post-separation arrangements (Maes et al, 2011). Taking part in decision-making about post-separation arrangements provided reassurance and helped children to accept the decisions made, ensuring that they felt 'appreciated and valued' (Smith et al, 2003, 207).

Good parental communication contributed to children's understandings of post-separation decisions as 'shared family problems', it supported children's ability to cope and increased the likelihood of the changes being accommodated (Moxnes, 2003; Bagshaw, 2007; Du Plooy and Van Rensburg, 2015; Morrison et al, 2017). It was particularly beneficial for those children who experienced multiple transitions (Flowerdew and Neale, 2003). Relationships are a central theme in children's experience of home after separation, invoking a sense of ease and comfort, a sense of belonging and shared interests with parents (and other household members) (Fehlberg et al, 2018). Children benefited from decisions which enabled them to maintain good relationships with both parents after separation. This was reflected in higher levels of accommodation (Moxnes, 2003; Hogan et al, 2003; Smith et al, 2003; Bagshaw, 2007; Fortin et al, 2012).

The next chapter focuses on parental conflict and its impact on children's accommodation of parental separation. Analysis of respondents' accounts allowed those children who experienced parental conflict to be identified. Chapter Nine (Conflict) considers its differential impact on children's experience according to whether it came to an end as a result of the separation or continued afterwards.

NINE

Conflict

Case study:
Catrina's story

Catrina (Respondent 17) is 19 years old, she was 12 when her parents separated. She found out by overhearing her parents arguing:

'My mum shouted at my dad, she said she had stopped loving him and was going.'

She describes how initially she 'thought the sky had fallen in'. She was 'quite religious and wanted God to make it all better'.

After her parents separated she hardly saw her mother for a while; this was because her parents could not agree on the living arrangements for her and her brothers. She recalls how her father

'kept telling us he would not let anyone take us away from him and he would always look after us. He always saw things as a fight with Mum to keep us so he used to remind us whenever we wanted to see Mum. He didn't think she could look after us on visits so it was hard and I thought I had to look after my brothers.'

And her mother

'could say some terrible things to Dad and sometimes to us. She said things she should not have said in front of us kids. I know they were upset but it's not fair on children and makes them feel bad and as if it's their fault.'

Because her parents could not agree on post-separation arrangements for the children, Catrina and her brothers spoke to a social worker 'and the courts had to sort it all out'. She felt able to talk to the social worker, and to her friends about her parents' separation but would have liked the opportunity to talk to a youth worker at that time:

'I think we all would have been better if we had seen some sort of youth worker who would have helped us not to bottle things up and get us to talk, that would have been better especially if my brothers would have spoken up more.'

Looking back, she describes how:

'At the time you have to get on with it, it can be worse now thinking back. But even then I knew that it was not fair that they made us feel like we did. Dad never hid that he did not like us seeing Mum and we all knew Mum hated Dad so it was hard going between the two.'

Catrina had a low level of accommodation.

A number of respondents experienced parental conflict in the course of their childhood, for some, the conflict related specifically to their parents' separation, for others it characterised their parents' relationship but subsided over time, while for others it continued after their parents separated. This chapter describes their experiences of parental conflict and examines how this affected their accommodation of parental separation.

The chapter started with Catrina's story, who was one of the respondents in this study. In describing her family experience, she provides an account of how parental conflict had an impact not only on her life as a child, but also as a young adult. Her experience provides insight into children's experiences of family relationships where there is a high level of parental conflict which persists until the present day. Unsurprisingly, given her experiences, her accommodation of parental separation was low.

As explained in Chapter Three (The research study), the questionnaire did not ask about parental conflict specifically, instead its presence was identified by scrutinising responses to questions asking respondents when they were told about their parents' separation (Question 7), whether there were any similarities between their experiences and the PSV (Question 6) and analysis of open text box comments.

Parental conflict emerged as a theme in 14 (1, 2, 5, 9, 10, 11, 17, 19, 21, 22, 24, 25, 28, 31) accounts and had been, or continued to be, an issue for 41 per cent of the respondents. In 12 cases respondents' levels of accommodation could be established but two (22, 24) lacked continuity.

Further analysis allowed respondents' experiences of parental conflict to be categorised according to whether parental conflict was specific to the time around parental separation, or whether it characterised their parents' relationship, but ended when their relationship ended, or whether it characterised their parents' relationship and continued after separation.

Three consistent findings emerged from their accounts: first, the negative impact of parental conflict on children's social and emotional wellbeing; second, the immediate and universal feelings of relief when conflict ended, and third, the higher levels of accommodation of parental separation found among those respondents who indicated parental conflict had ended.

Negative impact of parental conflict on children's social and emotional wellbeing

Many respondents described how conflict between their parents had had an impact on their lives. Often, they found about their parents' separation 'by overhearing their parents arguing', some went on to describe the high levels of anxiety this news and the subsequent changes, created:

> 'My anxiety levels increased to the point of having panic attacks. It would have been good to have more help with this, maybe from the GP.' (Respondent 11; aged 9–12)

> 'I was so upset and anxious that I developed an eating disorder and struggled with this for a long time. It was so bad that eventually I even thought about taking my own life. In those days eating disorders were not talked about quite so much and I think someone could have helped me get support more quickly. It was the worst time of my life.' (Respondent 31; aged 9–12)

For these respondents, their parents' separation coincided with the transition from primary to high school. Each referred to the introduction of a residential stepfather as part of post-separation changes, indicating that they faced a number of changes at this time.

A little older at the time her parents separated, Respondent 19 said that she knew that:

'Mum and Dad couldn't live together even though I wanted them to. It was obvious it was better for them to divorce. So even though it was really hard I knew everything would be better when they didn't live together and it would be OK in the end.' (Respondent 19; aged 13–16)

She described arguments about post-separation living arrangements and how she was drawn into them until her parents realised the effect this was having on her:

'My mum and dad could not agree on where we should live when they divorced and it caused lots of arguments. My mum was refusing to move out so Dad had to go and he was not happy. They argued a lot and involved me at first until they saw it was upsetting me because I cried a lot.' (Respondent 19; aged 13–16)

Another respondent (9), described the burden of being drawn into her parents' arguments and how she was used to relay messages between them. As an only child, she found this particularly difficult:

'It was really difficult, Mum and Dad had separated twice before but this time I knew it was final. Dad had stayed in the house before but Mum refused to move out this time and he was very angry. He caused problems throughout the divorce process despite the fact they agreed to divorce and that made Mum very angry. She would tell me all about how he was behaving and then when I saw Dad he would do the same about Mum. They wouldn't talk to each other and so used me to send messages to each other. It was really hard. I don't have any brothers or sisters and so there was no one else to share it.' (Respondent 9; aged 13–16)

For these four respondents, parental conflict was specific to the time around parental separation, once their parents separated and post-separation arrangements had been put in place, the conflict ended; each showed a high level of accommodation. Their accounts were in marked contrast to those who saw parental conflict as a key feature of their parents' relationship that continued after separation.

Gemma's (22) situation was described in the case study at the start of Chapter Six, she was aged 0–4 at the time of parental separation. She referred to parental conflict as well as the numerous changes that took place after separation with both parents going on to form new relationships almost immediately. Rather than focusing on how the conflict had affected her life, in her account she emphasised her confusion and the consequences for her and her brother as a result of the number and pace of changes. Her grandmother became a main source of support, and she went to live with her when she reached secondary school age. Her experience was in marked contrast to that of her brother who became 'aggressive and violent, was suspended from school and eventually expelled' eventually becoming a member of a gang and being imprisoned twice as a consequence of his offending.

Now aged 25, she explained how her childhood experiences have informed the way she raises her own children, in particular her commitment to avoiding the negative experiences she had. Her level of accommodation of parental separation was assessed as medium on account of the emotional distance she has placed between her childhood family experiences and the family experiences she had gone on to create.

Parental conflict was an on-going feature of the lives of two respondents (1, 17) even as young adults. Catrina's experience (17) was described in the case study at the beginning of this chapter. There were similarities between Catrina's and Respondent 1's experiences; both aged 9–12 at the time of separation, they experienced very high levels of conflict between their parents, were fully aware of their fathers' views that they should live with them and lost contact with their mothers for a while, until post-separation arrangements were determined by the courts. Their accounts described the emotional impact of being embroiled in their parents' conflict.

Respondent 1 recalled how she found out about her parents' separation by overhearing her parents arguing and her mother shouting that

'she didn't love him and was leaving'. (Respondent 1; aged 9–12)

Later, she said that:

'Dad said he was going to court to "keep us" and we saw a social worker. My dad saw it as a fight to keep us that he had to win.' (Respondent 1; aged 9–12)

After her parents separated, she lived with her father and siblings, but was aware that her father 'never wanted us to spend time with Mum because she left us. When we saw Mum there were lots of arguments about times and visiting. As the oldest I was a bit like mum to my brothers and sisters and felt like I had to look after them.' (Respondent 1; aged 9–12)

As she explained:

'It's really hard when your mum and dad hate each other. I suppose it's best if they split up, but I still get upset when I think about it. That hasn't got any easier because they still argue – in fact at the moment it's probably worse, I don't know why.' (Respondent 1; aged 9–12)

Each of these respondents (1,17) showed a low level of accommodation.

Parental conflict was not always experienced by witnessing arguments, sometimes children experienced parental conflict in a way that 'silenced' them from talking about their family relationships at home. This was the case for one male respondent (5), who lost contact with his father for a time and described how it was:

'hard not seeing Dad or hearing from him. Mum and my sisters were always having a go about Dad and I didn't feel I could mention his name at home.' (Respondent 5; aged 9–12)

He showed a medium level of accommodation.

Universal feelings of relief when conflict ended

The sense of relief respondents felt when parental conflict ended was universal and clearly articulated in some accounts. Respondent 24, aged 17–20 at the time of her parents' separation, described the immediate changes her parents' separation brought and referred to her father's departure in particularly positive terms. She was

'just relieved that it was all over now and we could finally start living.' (Respondent 24; aged 17–20)

'At last, they should have done it years ago! Life was so much better...Straight away, everything calmed down at home and we felt comfortable and calm.' (Respondent 24; aged 17–20)

She recalled meeting her father some time after the separation and telling him

> 'what it had felt like living at home at that time, how his behaviour had made us feel worthless and how badly he had treated Mum. He didn't want to listen. I haven't seen him since.' (Respondent 24; aged 17–20)

Her levels of satisfaction and acceptance lacked continuity.

Feeling frightened

Two respondents (10, 21), aged 9–12 at the time of separation, referred to 'being frightened', 'scared' or fearful during the time their parents lived together. One (21), made explicit reference to domestic violence and described how her parents' separation made her

> 'happier because of my dad being violent towards Mum'. (Respondent 21; aged 9–12)

It meant that she

> 'stopped being frightened at home'. (Respondent 21; aged 9–12)

She believed that her mother took her views into consideration in deciding to separate from her father because

> 'My mum knew I was getting scared and this made her leave Dad I think.' (Respondent 21; aged 9–12)

She acknowledged that at the time:

> 'Like anyone, I wanted Mum and Dad together, but deep down I knew that wasn't good for them and it would only get worse.' (Respondent 21; aged 9–12)

Since their separation, her relationship with each parent had improved, as had the relationship between her parents:

'We get on fine now and they are both much happier with their lives and are able to speak to each other.' (Respondent 21; aged 9–12)

Her account showed a high level of accommodation.

Domestic violence was a feature of Respondent 10's parents' relationship, also aged 9–12 at the time of their separation. She explained how their separation

'was a relief because of the way Dad behaved at home'. (Respondent 10; aged 9–12)

And how after her father left, she felt

'less scared and more relaxed'. (Respondent 10; aged 9–12)

She believed it was her 'fear'

'that finally made my mum leave Dad'. (Respondent 10; aged 9–12)

But she could recall a time when her parents' relationship had been different:

'Before my dad was aggressive and violent, we had been happy and I wanted that time to come back.' (Respondent 10; aged 9–12)

There was no explanation for the change in her father's behaviour, but over time family relationships had improved:

'Both my mum and dad are happy now and they are in good relationships and I get on with them both.' (Respondent 10; aged 9–12)

She showed a high level of accommodation.

These two respondents had a clear understanding of what family life was like when their parents lived together and that parental separation could only be viewed positively. After separation, domestic violence had ended and over time they had been able to establish positive relationships with each parent, it would be interesting to know more about what steps their parents took in helping them to achieve this.

Adjusting to post-separation changes

Sometimes the relief brought about by the end of parental conflict was tempered with feeling unsettled because of post-separation changes. This was evident in Respondent 25's account, who described how

> 'It was nice not to have all the rows and the uncomfortable silences, but at the same time it was unsettling because everything was different, where we went, who we saw and where we saw them. It was confusing having to live between two homes and my dad had a new girlfriend, so we had to get used to her.' (Respondent 25; aged 5–8)

As the eldest child she also felt a sense of responsibility towards her younger brother which she found stressful:

> 'As the oldest child I felt responsible for my brother and I worried about him a lot. When I think back I was very stressed and I was upset easily and started to pull my hair out which became a habit.' (Respondent 25; aged 5–8)

Over time, family relationships settled and she felt pleased that her parents had separated because relationships had improved. She showed a high level of accommodation.

On hearing of her parents' separation, Respondent 28's immediate response was of feeling

> 'relief and safe'. (Respondent 28; aged 9–12)

Her parents had separated previously, but

> 'got back together, she [Mum] had to pretend to be happy, but I don't really think she was. My father seemed to think he was the winner, because most of the children blamed Mum for the split...When my parents split, I knew what had happened and went with Mum. The younger ones didn't know what had happened and didn't know what Dad had done so they stayed and blamed Mum.' (Respondent 28; aged 9–12)

She explained her views had been taken into account in post-separation arrangements, but this resulted in her living with her mother, and her siblings living with her father. She felt the loss of daily contact with her siblings very keenly, this exerted a negative impact on her accommodation of the separation which was assessed as medium.

Family support

Many respondents identified family members who supported them during the time of their parents' separation and subsequently (see Chapter Seven), but only two made specific reference to how they had been supported in dealing with their parents' conflict.

Respondent 9 explained earlier how her parents drew her into their arguments by not talking to each other but telling her how the other was behaving and using her as a messenger. She found this hard and as an only child felt unable to share her experience; eventually she spoke to her aunt who then talked to her mother:

> 'Eventually my aunt had a word with my mum and she realised how I felt caught in the middle of their arguments. She spoke to Dad on that occasion and they both stopped. Mum has tried to make contact with Dad's family but it didn't work out – they made it clear they don't want anything to do with her. I find it difficult sometimes at family do's because I feel a loyalty to both and can feel torn.' (Respondent 9; aged 13–16)

In this case having listened to the aunt, her mother spoke to her father and positive change was brought about in the behaviour of each parent, changes resulting in a high level of accommodation.

Sometimes parents came to realise the impact their conflict was having on their child themselves, such as in Respondent 19's case who described arguments about the living arrangements for her and her siblings after separation earlier. Initially her parents involved her in their arguments until they came to recognise how distressing this was for her. No longer involved in their conflict, she felt able to draw on support from her mother, father, aunt and friends, although she did not feel able to talk to anyone about the separation. Recognising that her parents were unable to live together harmoniously and that it was better for them to separate influenced her thinking from the outset, she had a high level of accommodation.

Higher levels of accommodation of post-separation changes for those who indicated parental conflict had ended

In their accounts, 14 respondents indicated that parental conflict was a feature of their parents' relationship. Higher levels of accommodation were found among those who indicated that parental conflict had ended, either because parental conflict was specific to the time around parental separation (2, 11, 19, 22, 31) or it characterised their parents' relationship but ended when their relationship ended (10, 21, 24, 25). Six (10, 11, 19, 21, 25, 31) of these respondents had a high level of accommodation. They shared a sense of relief brought about by the end of parental conflict and all benefited either from the support of family members, or being able to talk to family or friends about their parents' separation.

Five respondents (1, 5, 9, 17, 28) experienced parental conflict which continued after separation, in two cases (1, 17) it continued to the present day. Levels of accommodation varied across this group according to whether parental conflict came to an end eventually, whether it subsided over time, or whether it persisted to the present day.

One (9) found her aunt's intervention brought about a positive change in the way her parents communicated meaning that they no longer drew her in to their arguments. In her case, parental conflict came to an end eventually and while she continued to feel a sense of 'divided loyalties' sometimes, her parents' decision to no longer involve her in their arguments and recognition that their separation was 'for the best' led to a high level of accommodation.

Two (5, 28) found that their parents' conflict subsided over time, but for Respondent 5 this involved the loss of contact with his father. Neither of these respondents were able to talk freely about their parents' separation: Respondent 5 because of the hostility expressed about his father by his mother and Respondent 28 because of her father's authoritarian parenting style:

> 'I had the sort of upbringing where I basically had to do as I was told…I knew that if I spoke about things that happened at home, and my dad found out, he would make me feel I had shamed the family.'

While they felt supported by family members they did not identify anyone to whom they could talk about the separation and although

Respondent 28's parents separated 11 years ago she had never spoken to anyone about it until taking part in this study:

> 'I am a quiet person and keep things to myself. I have never spoken about it before.' (Respondent 28; aged 9–12)

Both respondents experienced loss as a result of their parents' separation, loss of contact with his father (5) and loss of daily contact with her siblings (28). In each case the lack of opportunity to talk to others about their parents' separation left them isolated. They had a medium level of accommodation.

A clear sense of loss was evident in Respondent 2's account. By the age of 12, she had experienced parental separation twice; her parents separating in her early years leading to her living with her grandparents who then separated. It was this experience to which she referred in her account: it was her grandparents whom she had heard arguing. She did not refer to any siblings, identified no one as a source of support or as someone she could talk to about the separation, and as a result she appeared particularly isolated. Although 15 years had passed since her grandparents separated she still had a low level of accommodation.

For two respondents (1, 17), parental conflict persisted to the present day. Aware of their parents' negative views of each other, they were burdened by the conflict, particularly as their parents had been unable to put aside their differences in order to attend to their children's needs and make appropriate post-separation arrangements. As the eldest child, each respondent felt the need to take on responsibility for younger siblings and as a result, took on the mantle of adult responsibilities and appeared beset by adult concerns at a young age. The extent to which this affected their lives as young adults could be seen in their accounts, which demonstrated a low level of accommodation.

Discussion

The negative impact parental conflict had on respondents' social and emotional wellbeing, and the greater stress and anxiety these children faced was a consistent theme in respondents' accounts, findings which support earlier studies (Moxnes, 2003; Smith et al, 2003; Bagshaw, 2007; Fortin et al, 2012; Beasang et al, 2012; Birnbaum and Saini, 2012a). They faced some of the greatest challenges to their ability to cope with change, with sometimes the stress and anxiety manifesting itself in physical or mental health issues (see respondents 11, 13) (Flowerdew and Neale, 2003; Bagshaw, 2007).

In those cases where domestic violence and parental conflict ended following their parents' separation, children stopped feeling frightened at home and their feelings of relief were immediate and universal. Similar feelings were expressed when conflict continued for a short time after separation but then ended, often as a result of post-separation arrangements being finalised. These respondents (10, 21, 25) often reported improved relationships with their parent(s) and showed a high level of accommodation. Many recognised that their views had been taken into account, either through a parent's decision to separate (10, 21) or by prioritising their continued attendance at the same school (11, 31). Through these actions they saw that they 'mattered' to their parent(s) and were taken into account in decision-making about post-separation arrangements (Maes et al, 2001). Parental responsiveness and communication laid a 'strong foundation' for positive outcomes for the child in these cases (Francia and Millear, 2015).

Their experiences were in marked contrast to those who continued to be caught up in their arguments, where the 'corrosive effect of parental conflict' was evident (Fortin et al, 2012, p 322). These respondents (1, 17) were emotionally burdened by hearing criticism of one parent by the other and witnessing parents' arguments at contact handovers. They felt 'divided loyalties' as a result, which in all cases caused considerable distress, findings which are consistent with previous studies (Dunn and Deater-Deckard, 2001; Butler et al, 2002; Hogan et al, 2003; Moxnes, 2003; Smith et al, 2003; Smart, 2006; Bagshaw, 2007). Faced with such a situation, children had to choose between maintaining contact with both parents and negotiating their relationship with each or aligning themselves with one parent and ending contact with the other. Each strategy had drawbacks. Those seeking to maintain contact with both parents focused on strategies that enabled them to do this, requiring them to focus on their parents' needs and aspirations rather than their own concerns as they grew up leading them to feel 'they were quite without adult support as they navigated their own problems' (Smart, 2006, 166). On the other hand they were able to maintain a relationship with both parents no matter how difficult this was. While those who aligned themselves with one parent lost contact with the other, a situation they might come to regret in later adult life (Birnbaum and Saini, 2012a; Fortin et al, 2012a).

Where parents (1, 17, 25) were unable to put their differences aside in order to attend to their children's needs, older children often felt the need to take on responsibility for younger siblings due to their parents' poor parenting (Roth et al, 2014), resulting in a loss of their childhood (Birnbaum and Saini, 2012a). Conflict over contact and living arrangements was a particular 'source of pain and unhappiness' and can be seen in those cases where parents were unable or unwilling to set aside their differences and cooperate for the sake of their children, resulting in them having to meet with a social worker in order for the matter to be determined by the court (Smith et al, 2003, 206). These respondents experienced the most difficulty adjusting to post-separation changes, their accounts showed a low level of accommodation.

Sometimes, while aware of one parent's strong dislike of the other, respondents (5, 28) did not witness parental conflict directly because of loss of contact with the non-resident parent. In these circumstances, children felt uncomfortable talking about their non-resident parent at home because of the resident parent's anticipated hostile response and were effectively 'silenced' from talking about this relationship, placing a significant emotional burden on the child. These children tended to become isolated and could feel unsupported by adults, a situation reflected in lower levels of accommodation.

A key influence on children's experience of parental conflict was the availability of family support. Those who had access to sources of support within their family, through extended family members, particularly grandparents, could use this to positive effect in supporting their own coping strategies. It reduced their isolation and was particularly beneficial when other family members could see the effect parental conflict was having on a child and intervened to bring about change on the child's behalf (see Respondent 9). Those without access to such opportunities tended to record lower levels of accommodation.

In the last chapter of the book, Chapter Ten (Future directions), attention is turned to how the framework could be used to develop a more nuanced understanding of the ways in which children experience parental separation and accommodate post-separation changes over time. The chapter explores how the framework might be used by practitioners working to support children and young people experiencing parental separation. Consideration is given to who might be best placed to use the framework to support children and young people in this situation and how they might do this. Messages contained within the framework are also valuable to separating parents who are putting arrangements in place for their children therefore consideration is given to how the framework might be used by parents and practitioners working with them to understand how their actions and decisions can promote a higher level of accommodation for their children.

TEN

Future directions

The aim of the study was to give 'voice' to young adults' childhood experiences of parental separation, 'voices' largely absent from the literature to date; this book has been written to ensure that their 'voices' are heard. In articulating their 'voice', their experiences have been listened to, acknowledged and understood, the framework amplifies those experiences, affecting children's accommodation of parental separation and post-separation changes, presenting them in a readily accessible form.

This final chapter considers how the framework can be used to develop a more nuanced understanding of the ways in which children experience parental separation and accommodate changes over time. Set within the context of what young adults had to say about information that would have been useful to them at the time (Question 19), the chapter explores the value of the framework for practitioners working to support children. Consideration of who might be best placed to support children in schools and how they might do this, involves looking at the role of practitioners, the Personal, Social, Health and Economic (PSHE) curriculum in schools and peer support. The study highlighted issues raised for young adults when parental separation coincided with the move to higher education and so its use by support services in universities is also considered.

When separating, parents make decisions about post-separation arrangements, children are largely powerless and lack agency in this process, and so the chapter goes on to consider the value of the framework to parents and those working with them in encouraging a deeper understanding of how their actions, responses and decisions can promote a higher level of accommodation for their children. The chapter starts by considering what children saw as their support needs.

Support needs

Chapter Seven (Support) showed that most respondents with a high level of accommodation identified their parent(s) as sources of support and were able to talk to them about the separation. They found this support network sufficient and did not want the opportunity to speak to someone outside the family about the separation, although two respondents (11, 31), aged 9–12 at the time, who identified very high levels of anxiety leading to health issues, panic attacks (11) and an eating disorder and suicidal thoughts (31), thought that they may have benefited from such an opportunity.

Their experience was in marked contrast to those who had a medium level of accommodation, where only two respondents identified their resident parent as a source of support and none identified anyone to whom they could talk. Often combined with a loss of contact, these children lacked parental reassurance in accommodating the separation and post-separation changes. Most indicated that they would have liked the opportunity to talk to someone outside the family to address the loneliness they felt at the time (see comments by 22, 28 and 33 below).

Respondents who had a low level of accommodation saw their parents as sources of support, although sometimes this was in the context of on-going parental conflict (1, 17). Notably, parental separation coincided with life transitions for all respondents in this level – between primary and secondary school (1, 2, 17) or to higher education and independent living (12). All respondents in this level said that they would have liked the opportunity to talk to someone outside the family about their parents' separation. The impact of life transitions on accommodation of parental separation is an area worthy of further investigation in order to gain more detailed understanding of how this has an impact on children's emotional wellbeing and to explore the development of appropriate support strategies.

The ten respondents who identified the person to whom they would have liked to talk outside the family, suggested a teacher (16) or someone in school (2, 24), a youth worker (1, 17) or a counsellor (7, 12, 17), a few emphasised the need for such discussions to be 'in confidence' (1, 2, 12) (see Chapter Seven). The next section considers respondents' views on the role of schools.

The role of schools

Young adults held different views about the role of schools, some saw them as having a monitoring role with the opportunity to intervene and offer timely individual support:

> 'It would be good if schools were better trained to spot patterns changing in young peoples' lives and offer some counselling.' (Respondent 28; aged 9–12)

'It would have been good to have someone who could have stepped in at an early stage and helped us.' (Respondent 24; aged 17–20)

Another would have welcomed further information provided in PSHE lessons:

'It would have been good to have some information, maybe in PSHE at school, but I might have been too young to take much in.' (Respondent 23; aged 5–8)

While others would have welcomed the opportunity to talk to peers who had experienced parental separation:

'It would have been good to talk to someone going through the same stuff.' (Respondent 33; aged 13–16)

'It would help to know that lots of people go through the same sort of things.' (Respondent 22; aged 0–4)

One respondent, experiencing parental separation as he started university held a similar view:

'Although I know everyone's experience is different speaking to someone who had been through their parents separating would have helped me.' (Respondent 34; aged 17–20)

Peer support may have brought about realisation that their family situation could improve over time and provided reassurance:

'It would have been good to talk to other children who had seen their parents fighting at home so that they could tell me how things could improve.' (Respondent 21; aged 9–12)

'It would have helped if someone had told me that things could get better if they split up.' (Respondent 10; aged 9–12)

When looking at schools, consideration needs to be given to who might be best placed to work with and support children whose parents are separating, and to how they might best be supported. These issues are considered in the following section, which also explores opportunities for using the framework within schools.

The value of the framework for practitioners

Who?

Previous research, highlighting the social and emotional impact of parental separation on young people and its influence on educational outcomes, identified the need for further research on their experience in order to enable schools to respond more effectively to these young people and their families (Beausang et al, 2012). Earlier research indicated that children do not always see teachers as the best people to talk to about their parents' separation, they questioned their ability to help, feared being seen as having a 'problem' by their classmates (Wade and Smart, 2002), being the focus of 'unnecessary (and unwelcome) fuss' (Butler et al, 2003, 177) or lacked trust (Bagshaw, 2007). Sometimes teachers provided an important role in helping children cope (Du Plooy and Van Rensburg, 2015), but non-teaching staff were often seen as more approachable (Wade and Smart, 2002).

The impact of parental separation on children's emotional wellbeing does not form part of initial teacher training programmes, so teachers' knowledge, understanding and confidence in responding to such issues other than in a safeguarding context cannot be assumed. Nonetheless, staff in schools are aware of changes in a child's address, the quality of communication they have with their parents and the child's network of friends, factors which show a change in a child's circumstances and may highlight loss of contact with a parent or a child's increasing isolation. The framework shows that these factors are associated with a lower level of accommodation of parental separation and could act as an early indicator that a child may benefit from additional support. 'Flagging up' such possibilities requires a coordinated approach within school, between administrative staff, pastoral support and teaching staff, suggesting a whole school approach is more appropriate when delivering continuing professional development.

Pastoral staff working alongside Special Educational Needs Co-ordinators (SENCos) appear particularly well placed to work with children who may benefit from additional support in order to promote their social, emotional and mental health wellbeing. Taking the lead in home–school partnerships, they work at the intersection of home and school and have detailed knowledge of the child and the family's circumstances. Practitioners could use the framework as a therapeutic tool to support their work with the child; working alongside the child it could be used to encourage them to recognise their situation and understand how they feel about family relationships, acting as a basis for discussion and decision-making. In this way children could identify their own positioning on the framework and the steps which they might take to help themselves, such as initiating conversation about the separation with a parent, engaging in fun activities with friends such as listening to music, playing sport, talking to trusted others or immersing themselves in other individual activities such as art, reading or education (Butler et al, 2002; Wade and Smart, 2002; Brand et al, 2017). This work could be supported by the guidelines for professionals (psychologists, counsellors, social workers, teachers) working with children of parental divorce developed by Brand et al (2017). Enabling children to identify what they can do in response to their situation not only empowers them but also builds personal resilience.

Nonetheless, the child's situation is one of relative powerlessness, parents are the decision makers in their separation so therefore work may need to be undertaken with the whole family. Pastoral staff work in a multi-agency context, with professionals such as social workers, educational psychologists and counsellors from other agencies including Child and Adolescent Mental Health Services (CAMHS). The framework offers the opportunity to develop shared understandings of the child's situation and support the development of intervention strategies with the family across these professionals.

How?

Respondents who indicated that they would have liked the opportunity to talk to others at the time of their parents' separation highlighted the role of PSHE and peer support.

PSHE curriculum

The PSHE curriculum in schools offers opportunities to support children experiencing parental separation and changes in their family life, discussions about different types of families and family relationships provides children with information and creates space to discuss issues, providing a level of informal peer support to children. It is important that teachers recognise the complexity and diversity of family forms and that the curriculum reflects this (Beausang et al, 2012).

Recognising the need to update current curriculum guidance on the teaching of Sex and Relationship Education in English schools which was issued in 2000, the Department for Education in England (DfE) is currently involved in consultation on its proposals for teaching Relationships Education in primary schools and Relationships and Sex Education (RSE) in secondary schools as part of the Personal, Social, Health and Economic (PSHE) curriculum in all schools (DfE, 2000, 2017, 2018). The results of the consultation and DfE's response will be published in early 2019 prior to regulations being put before the Houses of Parliament for debate, if approved, statutory guidance will be issued later that year with all schools required to teach the new subjects from September 2020 (2018).

Under these proposals primary schools (age 4-11) will be required to provide Relationship Education but will retain choice on whether to teach age-appropriate sex education, Relationships and Sex Education (RSE) will be taught in all Secondary schools (age 11-16) (DfE, 2017).

Relationship Education in primary schools will focus on healthy relationships and as such 'will help those children who are experiencing or witnessing unhealthy relationships know where to seek help and support' (DfE, 2018, 10). The proposed subject content will focus on the following:

- Families and people who care for me
- Caring friendships
- Respectful friendships
- Online relationships
- Being safe (DfE, 2018, 11)

Building on content taught at primary level, the RSE curriculum at secondary school will draw 'in more content on unhealthy relationships and associated risks' and introduce 'content on intimate relationships and sex' (DfE, 2018, 11). The proposed subject content will focus on:

- Families
- Respectful relationships, including friendships
- Online and media
- Being safe
- Intimate and sexual relationships, including sexual health' (DfE, 2018, 11)

Parents will not be able to withdraw their child from Relationship Education in primary school or secondary school because 'this covers content all pupils should know to keep themselves safe and happy' (DfE, 2018, 12). In a proposed change to the current position, however, the government indicates that although parents will be able to request their child is withdrawn 'from some or all elements of sex education in RSE and this should be granted unless the headteacher, taking into account any considerations about the pupil and their circumstances, decides otherwise' this will end at the time when the child reaches three terms before they turn 16 (DfE, 2018, 12). At this point 'if the child wishes to receive sex education rather than be withdrawn, then the school should make arrangements to provide sex education during one of those terms' (DfE, 2018, 12). This change has been made to take account of young people's ability to consent and engage in sexual activity at the age of 16 and to ensure their opportunity to access sex education beforehand, as well as English case law and the European Convention on Human Rights (DfE, 2018).

The government also proposes introducing Health Education as a compulsory subject within the PSHE curriculum to sit alongside Relationships Education and RSE in order to support children's understanding of links between their physical and mental health (2018). The proposed subject content will focus on:

- Mental wellbeing
- Internet safety and harms
- Physical health and fitness
- Healthy eating
- Drugs and alcohol
- Health and prevention
- Basic first aid
- Changing adolescents' bodies (DfE, 2018, 15)

Discussing familes, respectful relationships, being safe and mental wellbeing will expose children to many ideas, providing the opportunity to explore their understanding of relationships and make sense of those around them. Responsive and sensitive teaching of this subject will support children in recognising that adult relationships are complex and change over time, that many children experience parental separation and despite changes in living arrangements their parents remain committed to them. Such an approach would have supported many of the children in this study. Additionally, when a need is identified in school, support in the form of the pastoral team, social workers and possibly Rainbows (see below) is available. However, delivering effective Relationships and Sex Education requires particular skills and there are indications some young adults believe that the subject is best delivered by specialist staff from outside schools working alongside staff in schools rather than by class or form teachers (Kay-Flowers and Faludi, 2016; 2017).

Peer support

Respondents emphasised the value of peer support in supporting children and young adults in adjusting to the changes brought about by their parents' separation. They thought that knowing how others experienced parental separation and that they faced similar issues could help. The opportunity to talk to peers can reduce loneliness; talking to others who have similar experiences can be a source of comfort and enable children to recognise how their situation is likely to improve over time (Butler et al, 2003; Hogan et al, 2003; Halpenny et al, 2008). This may have been a useful strategy to support those boys in this study who lost contact with their fathers after separation and were unlikely to talk to people outside the family.

The Rainbows programme is a peer support programme that supports children and young people who have experienced a significant loss through death, relationship breakdown or other adverse circumstance (Hutchings, 2011). Delivered by trained facilitators in schools, it uses a range of activities to foster a supportive environment for children. The facilitators are usually employed by the school, but are not always teachers, thereby providing continuity and support for children outside the sessions, but overcoming the concerns expressed by children in Wade and Smart's (2002) study. Children involved in the programme often feel reassured to find that others share the experience of parental separation and gain confidence in talking about their feelings, and practitioners and parents find it an effective approach in supporting children through parental separation (Halpenny et al, 2008; Hutchings, 2011).

This framework could be used by practitioners working in similar group settings or facilitating peer support as a basis for discussion and development of personal strategies. The case study scenarios described in this book could be used to support such work.

A role for universities

In the study two respondents explained how their experience of parental separation coincided with their move to university and independent living; they felt overwhelmed by the situation and lacked support. Living away from home in a new location without easy access to their existing friendship groups highlighted their vulnerability. They were shocked by the decision, anxious about what was happening at home and found it difficult to concentrate on their studies, often feeling 'torn' between their new life and their home life, the timing and pace of changes presented particular challenges to their coping (Flowerdew and Neale, 2003; Cooper Sumner, 2013; Abetz and Wang, 2017). Their experiences highlight the important role of student support services in universities and the need for these services to be well publicised within the student population.

They indicated that talking to others, particularly those who had gone through their parents' separation would have been beneficial and it may be that peer support in the form of informal support groups may be helpful (Morrison et al, 2017). There is potential for this framework to be used by student services when working with young adults in similar circumstances in order to help them understand their own family situation, identify their support needs and develop appropriate coping strategies. Such work could be undertaken on an individual basis or in a group context, depending on the student's needs.

Other settings

Consideration has been given to practitioners' use of the framework in educational settings, namely schools and universities, but it could be used in a similar way by staff working with children and families in Children's Services, Children's Centres and Family Support Centres. Its use could also be considered in informal education settings such as youth clubs and youth centres. However, it would benefit from further adaptation into a more child friendly version for use with younger children.

The value of the framework for families

Parents

There were three parents in the study, and while being a parent did not necessarily influence their level of accommodation, childhood experiences did influence the way they parented. They had very different experiences of parental separation, but each had a difficult relationship with their father, and parental separation involved the loss of contact for two (20, 29) which they viewed as a positive development. There was evidence that the childhood experiences of the two mothers (20, 22) acted as a moral compass in the way that they responded to their own children: in the decision to prevent her child having contact with her grandfather (20), and in listening to her children and prioritising their needs (22) (Smart, 2006). The one father (29) in the study was experiencing difficulties in his second marriage but aimed to improve the situation for his children's benefit. In each case, these parents aspired to be more child centred in their approach to parenting.

Gemma (22) (case study in Chapter Six) was of the opinion that people needed support and that classes about getting married and raising children may be beneficial.

> 'I suppose it's different for each family but I think people need support and maybe classes about getting married and how to bring up children. That would mean that the children get listened to instead of it being all about the adults.' (Respondent 22; aged 0–4)

Further investigation into the attitudes young adults who experienced parental separation have towards their future role as parents and expectations of parenting might usefully inform the content of such classes and allow any support needs to be identified. In the meantime, revision of the Sex and Relationship Education (SRE) curriculum at least offers the prospect that discussion of intimate and family relationships will provide a context for considering expectations in preparation for when young adults embark on their own relationships and become parents themselves.

Working with parents

The framework provides an accessible way for parents to understand factors and experiences influencing children's accommodation of parental separation and post-separation changes over time and recognise their own child's situation within the family. Used by practitioners as an awareness-raising tool, it would enable parents to assess the current position, consider areas where they might support their child in improving their satisfaction and acceptance of post-separation changes and identify strategies to enable their child to reach the highest possible level of accommodation. Work undertaken by Morrison et al (2017), suggesting ways in which therapists might work with divorcing parents, and by Fehlberg et al (2018) on children's experience of home after parental separation, would support its use.

The framework encourages parents to focus on their child's needs, to listen to their children and adopt a child-centred approach. Used as the basis of discussion with practitioners, it encourages parents to talk to their children about what is happening in the family, to ensure that their children feel that they 'matter' in post-separation arrangements and provides the prospect of reassurance for parents that they are acting in a way that supports their children in accommodating post-separation changes in the long term.

The opportunity exists for professionals working with parents to use it to reinforce the messages of young adults who experienced parental separation in childhood that a child-centred approach and the actions parent(s) take to support this, encourage a higher level of accommodation in the long term. Used in this way, the framework could have wide application in work undertaken by different agencies including Children's Services, Children and Family Court Advisory and Support Service (CAFCASS) and those in the voluntary sector, such as Gingerbread (supporting single parents) and Relate (which provides relationship support, including counselling for children and young people).

The framework could be used independently by parent(s) seeking to resolve issues for themselves, or alongside other tools such as 'The Parenting Plan', in which parents set out a shared commitment to their children and their future, recording decisions about communication, living arrangements, money, religion, education, healthcare and emotional wellbeing (CAFCASS, 2015a).

Faced with their own issues and particular concerns at the time of separation, not all parents feel that they have the knowledge and skills required to support their child at that time; practitioners can have an important role in encouraging and supporting them. Parenting classes may offer space and time for reflection and provide the opportunity for alternative models of parenting to be considered. The Separated Parents Information Programme (SPIP), delivered by a network of voluntary organisations on behalf of CAFCASS is one example; working solely with separated parents, this short programme focuses on the best interests of the child, what children need, parental communication and emotions (2015b). Family courts have the power to direct parents to attend the programme. Based on young adults' views of their childhood experience of parental separation, the framework might provide a useful focus within such programmes.

The diversity of families' needs requires a variety of approaches. In some cases, parents need support in maintaining or renewing positive family relationships, particularly after the loss of contact. There may be a need for the parent to 'reconnect' with their child, in which case 'bonding sessions' between the child and parent may be suggested to enhance parental communication, or a parent may need to develop understanding of attachment and loss to support decision-making about post-separation arrangements. Such work is undertaken by local authority Children's Services, Family Support Centres and voluntary sector agencies. The framework would provide a useful addition to their existing toolkit for working with children and families and could be used as an awareness-raising tool or to support appropriate strategies to enable their child to reach the highest level of accommodation.

Future direction

The starting point for these considerations is to engage in professional dialogue with interested practitioners, to see how the framework relates to their experience of separating or separated parents and to explore ways in which it might be used as a therapeutic tool in their work with children and parents. Exploratory discussions should focus on the framework and interpreting the different levels of accommodation in order to consider its value as a tool in aiding children's understanding of their family situation and in identifying strategies that will support them in accommodating change. Such discussions will also consider its value as a tool for parents, to support them in recognising and responding to their children's needs. The target audience for these discussions will be practitioners working in schools, staff working in student support services in universities and practitioners engaged in family support work.

Conclusion

When parental separation occurs in childhood, it leads to permanent changes in family relationships, family structures and family dynamics, and there can be no return to the family arrangements children previously experienced. Children are required to adjust to living in a different family structure, to new living arrangements, the loss of daily contact with one parent, sometimes the loss of contact entirely, maybe the introduction of new people into their family as well as changes in practical arrangements such as where they live and the school they attend. These are changes which children have not sought, may not necessarily want and in which they have little or no say.

Giving 'voice' to young adults' childhood experiences of parental separation has increased understanding of how some felt about the separation and post-separation changes at the time. With the passage of time these young adults were able to reflect on their childhood experiences, consider what happened, the changes that took place and to re-evaluate events. The findings support those of earlier studies, highlighting the importance of children having good communication with each parent and the role of parental support in encouraging a higher level of accommodation of parental separation and the changes it brings (Dunn and Deater-Deckard, 2001; Butler et al, 2002; Hogan et al, 2003; Moxnes, 2003; Bagshaw, 2007; Maes et al, 2011; Fortin et al, 2012; Brand et al, 2017; Morrison et al, 2017). Their experiences were in contrast to those children whose parents did not communicate or support them and where contact with a parent may have been lost; over time these children created emotional distance and showed a medium level of accommodation. Young adults who continued to experience parental conflict despite the separation occurring some time ago described the negative impact the conflict exerted on their lives and found difficulty seeing how their needs were recognised. They had the lowest level of accommodation (Dunn and Deater-Deckard, 2001; Butler et al, 2002; Flowerdew and Neale, 2003; Moxnes, 2003; Smart, 2006; Smith et al, 2003; Bagshaw, 2007; Fortin et al, 2012; Brand et al, 2017). These experiences might also have implications for their future romantic relationships (Morrison et al, 2017).

Their youthfulness meant that most respondents experienced these events relatively recently. Their transition to young adulthood enabled them to exercise agency in their lives and achieve some distance, which provided the opportunity for considered reflection. The study shows that when parental separation is handled sensitively and children are supported over time they accommodate parental separation and life after separation well. It illustrates the importance of parents adopting a child-centred approach, where children's interests are at the centre of post-separation considerations.

Their perspective offers unique insights into what is important to children when their parents are separating and shows how parents' actions and responses can bring about a higher level of accommodation of post-separation changes over time. Young adults' 'voice' on childhood experiences of parental separation holds valuable messages for children, for parents and for practitioners. These are encapsulated in the framework and its use offers the opportunity for their 'voices' to influence the actions of others. The value of the framework lies as a tool for aiding children and young people's understanding of their family situation, enabling them to identify strategies that will support them in accommodating change. Its aim is to support children, to encourage them to access support and talk to those they can trust and enable parents to recognise actions which they can take to support their children in reaching the highest level of accommodation possible, such that one day their child may be able to say:

> 'Now that I am older I see it differently. My family are close…I am glad that my parents have separated because we like each other more and respect each other.' (Respondent 25; aged 5–8)

References

AOIR (Association of Internet Researchers) (2012) *Ethical Decision-Making and Internet Research: Recommendations from the AOIR Ethics Working Committee (Version 2.0)*, http://aoir.org/reports/ethics2.pdf

Abetz, J, Wang, TR (2017) '"Were they ever really happy the way that I remember?": Exploring sources of uncertainty for adult children of divorce', *Journal of Divorce and Remarriage*, doi: 10.1080/10502556.2017.1301158

Bagnoli, A, Clark, A (2010) 'Focus groups with young people: A participatory approach to research planning', *Journal of Youth Studies*, 13 (1): 101–119

Bagshaw, D (2007) 'Reshaping responses to children when parents are separating: Hearing children's voices in the transition', *Australian Social Work*, 60 (4): 450–465

Beausang, J, Farrell, A, Walsh, K (2012) 'Young people whose parents are separated or divorced: A case for researching their experiences at the intersection of home and school', *Educational Research*, 54 (3): 343–356, doi: 10.1080/00131881.2012.710092

BERA (British Educational Research Association) (2011) *Ethical Guidelines for Educational Research*, London: BERA

Birnbaum, R, Saini, M (2012a) 'A scoping review of qualitative studies about children experiencing parental separation', *Childhood*, 20: 260–282, doi: 10.1177/0907568212454148

Birnbaum, R, Saini, M (2012b) 'A qualitative synthesis of children's participation in custody disputes', *Research on Social Work Practice*, 22: 400–409

Birnbaum, R, Bala, N, Cyr, F (2011) 'Children's experience with family justice professionals in Ontario and Ohio', *Journal of Law, Policy and the Family*, 25: 398–422

Brand, C, Howcroft, G, Hoelson, CM (2017) 'The voice of the child in parental divorce: Implications for clinical practice and mental health practitioners', *Journal of Child & Adolescent Mental Health*, 29 (2): 169–178, doi: 10.2989/17280583.2017.1345746

Butler, I, Scanlan, L, Robinson, M, Douglas, G, Murch, M (2002) 'Children's involvement in their parents' divorce: Implications for practice', *Children & Society*, 16: 89–102

Butler, I, Scanlan, L, Robinson, M, Douglas, G, Murch, M (2003) *Divorcing Children*, London: Jessica Kingsley

CAFCASS (Children and Family Court Advisory and Support Service) (2015a) *The Parenting Plan*, www.cafcass.gov.uk/grown-ups/parents-and-carers/resources-parents-carers/

CAFCASS (Children and Family Court Advisory and Support Service) (2015b) *Separated Parents Information Programme Factsheet*, www.cafcass.gov.uk/grown-ups/parents-and-carers/resources-parents-carers/

Campbell, A (2008) 'The right to be heard: Australian children's views about their involvement in decision-making following parental separation', *Child Care in Practice*, 14 (3): 237–255

Cashmore, J, Parkinson, P (2008) 'Children's and parents' perceptions on children's participation in decision-making after separation and divorce', *Family Court Review*, 46: 91–104

Clough, P, Nutbrown, C (2012) *A Student's Guide to Methodology* (3rd edn), London: Sage

Cohen, L, Manion, L, Morrison, K (2011) *Research Methods in Education* (7th edn), Abingdon: Routledge

Cohen, L, Manion, L, Morrison, K (2018) *Research Methods in Education* (8th edn), Abingdon: Routledge

Cooper Sumner, C (2013) 'Adult children of divorce: Awareness and intervention', *Journal of Divorce & Remarriage*, 54 (4), 271–281, doi: 10.1080/10502556.2013.780461

Denscombe, M (2014) *The Good Research Guide* (5th edn), Maidenhead: Open University Press

Denscombe, M (2017) *The Good Research Guide* (6th edn), Maidenhead: Open University Press

Denzin, NK, Lincoln, YS (2011) 'Introduction: The discipline and practice of qualitative research', in NK Denzin, YS Lincoln (eds) *The Sage Handbook of Qualitative Research*, London: Sage

DfE (Department for Education for England) (2000) *Sex and Relationship Education Guidance*, July, Ref: DFEE 0116/2000, London: DfE, www.dfe.gov.uk

DfE (2017) *Policy Statement: Relationships Education, Relationships and Sex Education and Personal, Social, Health and Economic Education*, March, London: DfE, www.dfe.gov.uk

DfE (2018) Relationships education, relationships and sex education, and health education in England, Government consultation (including call for evidence response), Launch date 19 July 2018, Respond by 7 November 2018. Available at: https://consult.education.gov.uk/pshe/relationships-education-rse-health-education/

Dowling, M, Cooney, A (2012) 'Research approaches related to phenomenology: negotiating a complex landscape', *Nurse Researcher*, 20 (2): 21–27

Du Plooy, K, Van Rensburg, E (2015) 'Young adults' perception of coping with parental divorce: A retrospective study', *Journal of Divorce and Remarriage*, 56 (6), 490–512, doi: 10.1080/10502556.2015.1058661

Dunn, J, Deater-Deckard, K (2001) *Children's Views of Their Changing Families*, York: Joseph Rowntree Foundation

Farrow, R, Arnold, P (2003) 'Changes in female student sexual behaviour during the transition to university', *Journal of Education Policy*, 21 (1), 59–74

Fehlberg, B, Natalier, K, Smyth, BM (2018) 'Children's experiences of "home" after parental separation', *Child and Family Law Quarterly*, 30 (1): 3–21

Finlay, L (2009) 'Debating phenomenological research methods', *Phenomenology and Practice*, 3 (1): 6–25

Flowerdew, J, Neale, B (2003) 'Trying to stay apace: Children with multiple challenges in their post-divorce family lives', *Childhood*, 10: 147–161, doi: 10.1177/0907568203010002003

Fortin, J, Hunt, J, Scanlan, L (2012) *Taking a Longer View of Contact: The Perspectives of Young Adults who Experienced Parental Separation in their Youth*, Sussex: Sussex Law School, University of Sussex

Francia, L, Millear, P (2015) 'Mastery or misery: Conflict between separated parents a psychological burden for children', *Journal of Divorce & Remarriage*, 56 (7), 551–568, doi: 10.1080/10502556.2015.1080090

Hadfield, M, Haw, K (2001) '"Voice", young people and action research', *Educational Action Research*, 9 (3), 485–502, doi: 10.1080/09650790100200165

Halling, S (2008) *Intimacy, Transcendence and Psychology: Closeness and Openness in Everyday Life*, New York: Palgrave Macmillan

Halpenny, AM, Greene, S, Hogan, D (2008) 'Children's perspectives on coping and support following parental separation', *Child Care in Practice*, 14 (3), 311–325

Heath, S, Brooks, R, Cleaver, E, Ireland, E (2009) *Researching Young People's Lives*, London: Sage

Hogan, DM, Halpenny, AM, Greene, S (2003) 'Change and continuity after parental separation: Children's experiences of family transitions in Ireland', *Childhood*, 10: 163–180, doi: 10.1177/0907568203010002004

Hutchings, N (2011) *An Evaluation of the Direct Impact of the Rainbows Programme in Supporting Children and Young people in Schools within South Yorkshire*, Luton: Rainbows Bereavement Support Great Britain

James, A (2007) 'Giving voice to children's voices: Practices and problems, pitfalls and potentials', *American Anthropologist*, 109 (2), 261–272

Jarrett, R, Odoms-Young, A (2013) 'Now that I have it, what do I do with it? Exploring techniques for interpreting, writing up and evaluating qualitative data workshop', *International Congress of Qualitative Inquiry 2013*, Urbana-Champaign, IL: University of Illinois

Kay, S (2006) 'Where do very young children and their parents derive support during parental separation?', *Family Court Journal*, 4 (1): 29–35

Kay-Flowers, S (2014) *Recalling Childhood Experiences of Parental Separation and Divorce: An Internet Based Phenomenology of Young Adult Voices*, PhD thesis, Sheffield: University of Sheffield, https://etheses. whiterose.ac.uk

Kay-Flowers, S, Faludi, C (2016) 'An exploration of attitudes towards sex and relationship education in UK and Romania: Implications for educational practice', paper presented at *Children and Young People in a Changing World International Conference*, 23 June, Liverpool: Liverpool Hope University

Kay-Flowers, S, Faludi, C (2017) 'Sex and relationship education in schools: Young adults' views on their experience and suggestions for change', paper presented at *International Interdisciplinary Conference on Childhood and Youth*, 28–30 June, Bangor: Bangor University

Keenan, T, Evans, S (2009) *An Introduction to Child Development* (2nd edn), London: Sage

Kinchloe, JL, McLaren, P, Steinberg, SR (2011) 'Critical pedagogy and qualitative research: Moving to the bricolage', in NK Denzin, YS Lincoln (eds) *The Sage Handbook of Qualitative Research*, London: Sage

Layard, R, Dunn, J (2009) *A Good Childhood*, London: Penguin

Maes, SDJ, De Mol, J, Buysse, A (2011) 'Children's experiences and meaning construction on parental divorce: A focus group study', *Childhood*, 19 (2): 266–279

Markham, A, Stravrova, S (2016) 'Internet/digital research', in D Silverman (ed) *Qualitative Research*, London: Sage

Marschall, A (2014) 'Who cares for whom? Revisiting the concept of care in the everyday life of post-divorce families', *Childhood*, 21 (4), 517–531.

Menning, CL (2008) '"I've kept it that way on purpose": Adolescents' management of negative parental relationship traits after divorce and separation', *Journal of Contemporary Ethnography*, 37: 586–618, doi: 10.1177/0891241607310545

Morrison, SC, Fife, ST, Hertlein, KM (2017) 'Mechanisms behind prolonged effects of parental divorce: A phenomenological study', *Journal of Divorce & Remarriage*, 58 (1), 44–63, doi: 10.1080/10502556.2016.1262652

Moxnes, K (2003) 'Risk factors in divorce: Perceptions by the children involved', *Childhood*, 10: 131–146, doi: 10.1177/0907568203010002002

NISRA (Northern Ireland Statistics and Research Agency) (2011) *Registrar General Annual Report 2010*, November, www.nisra.gov.uk/publications/registrar-general-annual-report-2001-2010

NISRA (Northern Ireland Statistics and Research Agency) (2012) *Registrar General Annual Report 2011*, November, https://www.nisra.gov.uk/publications/registrar-general-annual-reports-2011-2015

NISRA (Northern Ireland Statistics and Research Agency) (2013) *Registrar General Annual Report 2012*, November, https://www.nisra.gov.uk/publications/registrar-general-annual-reports-2011-2015

NISRA (Northern Ireland Statistics and Research Agency) (2014) *Registrar General Annual Report 2013*, November, https://www.nisra.gov.uk/publications/registrar-general-annual-reports-2011-2015

NISRA (Northern Ireland Statistics and Research Agency) (2015) *Registrar General Annual Report 2014*, July, https://www.nisra.gov.uk/publications/registrar-general-annual-reports-2011-2015

NISRA (Northern Ireland Statistics and Research Agency) (2016) *Registrar General Annual Report 2015*, August, www.nisra.gov.uk/publications/registrar-general-annual-reports-2011-2015

ONS (Office for National Statistics) (2014) *Dependent Children Usually Resident in England and Wales with a Parental Second Address*, 25 July, https://tinyurl.com/ybvpy2n4

ONS (Office for National Statistics) (2015) *Divorces in England and Wales: Children of Divorced Couples*, 23 November, www.ons.gov.uk/peoplepopulationandcommunity/birthsdeathsandmarriages/divorce/datasets/divorcesinenglandandwaleschildrenofdivorcedcouples

ONS (Office for National Statistics) (2017a) *Freedom of Information Request: UK Population 2017*, 20 July, www.ons.gov.uk/aboutus/transparencyandgovernance/freedomofinformationfoi/ukpopulation2017

ONS (Office for National Statistics) (2017b) *Families and Households in the UK: 2017*, Statistical Bulletin, 8 November, www.ons.gov.uk/peoplepopulationandcommunity/birthsdeathsandmarriages/families/bulletins/familiesandhouseholds/2017

ONS (Office for National Statistics) (2017c) *Freedom of Information Request: Number of Separated Families in the UK*, 5 October, www.ons.gov. uk/aboutus/transparencyandgovernance/freedomofinformationfoi/ numberofseparatedfamiliesintheuk

ONS (Office for National Statistics) (2017d) *Divorces in England and Wales: 2016*, https://tinyurl.com/y7rdumjb

Orgad, S (2005) *Storytelling Online: Talking Breast Cancer on the Internet*, New York: Peter Lang

Orgad, S (2009) 'How can researchers make sense of the issues involved in collecting and interpreting online and off-line data?', in AN Markham, NK Baym (eds) *Internet Inquiry: Conversations about Method*, London: Sage

Quigley, C, Cyr, F (2018) 'The voice of the child in parenting coordination: Views of children, parents and parenting coordinators', *Journal of Divorce & Remarriage*, 59 (6), doi: 10.1080/10502556.2017.1403823

Robson, C (2011) *Real World Research* (3rd edn), Chichester: John Wiley and Sons

Rodgers, B, Pryor, J (1998) *Divorce and Separation: The Outcomes for Children*, York: Joseph Rowntree Foundation

Roth, KE, Harkins, DA, Eng, LA (2014) 'Parental conflict during divorce as an indicator of adjustment and future relationships: A retrospective sibling study', *Journal of Divorce & Remarriage*, 55 (2), 117–138, doi: 10.1080/10502556.2013.871951

Scottish Government (2017) *Civil Justice Statistics in Scotland 2015–2016*, Main Tables, 2015–16, www.gov.scot/Publications/2017/03/5915/7

Smart, C (2003) 'Introduction: New perspectives on childhood and divorce', *Childhood*, 10, 123–129, doi: 10.1177/0907568203010002001

Smart, C (2006) 'Children's narratives of post-divorce family life: From individual experience to an ethical disposition', *The Sociological Review*, 54 (1): 155–170

Smith, AB, Taylor, NJ, Tapp, P (2003) 'Rethinking children's involvement in decision-making after parental separation', *Childhood*, 10: 201–216, doi: 10.1177/0907568203010002006

Spyrou, S (2011) 'The limits of children's voices: From authenticity to critical, reflexive representation', *Childhood*, 18 (2): 151–165

Wade, A, Smart, C (2002) *Facing Family Change: Children's Circumstances, Strategies and Resources*, York: Joseph Rowntree Foundation

Whitty, MT, Joinson, AN (2009) *'Truth, Lies and Trust on the Internet'*, Hove: Routledge

Wolgemuth, JR, Erdil, Z, Opsal, T, Cross, J, Kaante, T, Dickmann, E, Colomer, S, (2013) '"There are no known benefits…": Participants' experiences of the qualitative interview', paper presented at *International Congress of Qualitative Inquiry* 2013, Urbana-Champaign, IL: University of Illinois

Case study for prompt simulation video (PSV)

There are three children (aged 11, 12 and 14) whose parents have recently separated. Mum has moved out of the family home into new accommodation taking the children with her. Dad would like all three children to live with him in the family home. Both parents believe the children need to live together but believe they would be best placed with them.

The parental relationship has always been volatile with frequent arguments sometimes culminating in plates being smashed. The children have learned that when their parents argue it is best to get out of the way quickly. Usually they take refuge in their bedrooms, this means that they have been able to hear what is going on and have sometimes seen their parents with a black eye or deep scratches on their arms the following day. Once they were so fearful that one of the children, Rebecca, contacted a neighbour who called the police to the house, their parents were warned about their behaviour and its damaging effect on the children but no charges were brought as a result of the incident.

Prior to the separation, their parents' arguments became more frequent and they overheard comments indicating mum had started to see someone else. After that the atmosphere in the house was very tense, their parents did not speak to each other, instead passing messages via the children, a pattern which has continued since separation. It was a very difficult time and initially there was considerable relief when their parents separated. They were reluctant to move with mum, but they felt they had to; dad was so upset at the time that he was unable to look at the bigger picture and therefore did not prevent them leaving.

Since then the children have had contact with dad, the nature and frequency of which has differed from child to child. He lives near to their school so they are able to visit him easily. While it is agreed that the children should see their dad if they want to, there is a dispute about its frequency and nature. The two younger children do not always tell mum when they see him after school for fear of her reaction and they are very anxious about telling her about the forthcoming week-long camping trip dad is planning.

Mum has continued with her new relationship and her new partner is a regular visitor to her home. The children have different responses to this arrangement.

Each child's response

Natasha is 14 years old and in year 10 at school

She sees herself as 'grown up' and her friends are an important source of comfort and support to her, consequently she is choosing to spend more time with them. She has always had a close relationship with mum who often confides in her. She is aware of the difficulties within her parents' marriage and sees her dad as being to blame. She gets on well with mum's new partner and is happy to spend time with him. She has seen her dad once since they left the family home and has said that she doesn't want to see him anymore because 'of all the bad stuff he did to Mum'. She cannot see why her brother and sister should want to see him either and tells them so.

Rebecca is 12 years old and in year 8 at school

Rebecca is finding it very hard to adjust to the changed family situation. She would like things to go back to the way they were with everyone living together, but without the arguments. She has always 'got on well' with both her parents, but now they are separated she hates the feeling that she always has to choose between them. If she spends time with dad she feels she is letting her mum and sister down, and if she is with mum she worries about her dad being on his own and the difficulties her brother might experience in seeing dad. She really feels that she is in a 'no win' situation and there is no way through. She appears distracted in school and her school work has begun to suffer, when one of her teachers raised this with her, she shared the problems she was having at home with them. The teacher suggested that she might want to see a counsellor, but Rebecca is aware that in order for this to happen the school will contact her parents and she is worried about their response, particularly as neither parent has advised the school of the family situation. She is aware of the impact the family situation is having on her because she often finds it difficult to sleep at night, to concentrate in school and her friends have noted how she 'is no fun anymore'.

Andrew is 11 years old and in year 7 at school

Andrew is in his first year at high school and appears to have settled in well. He moved to this school with a large group of children from primary school. He plays the saxophone and is involved in the chess club. He finds PE daunting because he is a little overweight and was teased about this at primary school. His interest in music is shared with dad and they have always spent a lot of time together as a result. He misses his dad enormously and would move to live with him if he could and ideally if Rebecca moved with him as well. He finds mum's new partner overwhelming because he 'tries too hard'. He disagrees with Natasha's view of the situation, but avoids talking to her about it.

Actors' script for prompt simulation video (PSV)

Character analysis

Natasha

Natasha is 14 years old, in year 10 at school. She is a confident, independent, mature young lady who spends time with friends and has a strong relationship with mum. She has a clear understanding of mum and dad's conflict, has a good relationship with mum's new boyfriend, Tommy, and doesn't want to see dad, in support of mum. She has seen dad once since they split and doesn't want to see dad anymore because 'of all the bad stuff he did to Mum'. She finds the conflict with her younger sister and brother difficult as she feels she must support them and none of them should see their dad.

Rebecca

Rebecca is 12 years old, in year 8 at school. She is very down and lacking in confidence, unhappy with the family situation and feels torn between her parents. She doesn't want to choose between them and would prefer it if they could sort out the family problems and be together again. She shows the characteristics of middle child syndrome, and there are reports from school of her becoming withdrawn and sad. Teachers suggested her speaking to a counsellor, but Rebecca is too scared as she knows her parents will be contacted about the situation. Rebecca is also having trouble sleeping at night and her friends have described her as 'no fun anymore'. There is conflict with her older sister who supports mum and has closed dad out.

Andrew

Andrew is 11 years old, in year 7 at school. He is a shy, self-conscious boy. He is slightly overweight which resulted in him being bullied at primary school and he finds PE difficult. He has strong musical interests and plays the saxophone, he is also in the school chess club and appears to be settling into school well. Andrew has a strong relationship with his father partly due to his musical interests. He misses his dad greatly and would prefer to live with him if his sister Rebecca would move as well. He dislikes mum's new boyfriend, Tommy, as he feels he tries too hard and makes Andrew feel uncomfortable. Andrew finds it very difficult to discuss the problems with his sisters – particularly Natasha – and avoids talking about the situation.

Scene one

Three children: Natasha (14), Rebecca (12), Andrew (11) are sitting together in the living room, around the kitchen table. Discussion: regarding current family situation.

Natasha: I don't understand, why would you still want to see Dad after everything he's done to Mum?

Rebecca: He's still our dad, and it isn't just his fault, it's no one's fault, but we should still be able to see our dad, I miss him…why can't we just all be together again?!

Natasha: Well what do you think Andrew, do you want to see Dad?

Andrew: [shy and quiet, refuses to answer]

Rebecca: Leave him alone, we want to see Dad. I don't know why you won't, but it's not your choice – it's ours.

Scene two

Individual camera shots: speaking about the situation between mum and dad.

Natasha: [confidently spoken] I don't get Becky and Andy, they don't understand you see, 'cos they're younger than me. Mum and Dad aren't meant to be together, we can't live like that anymore, it's too hard for all of us. Tommy, mum's new boyfriend, is great, he makes her happy and treats her well, I just wish they could see that. I've seen what Dad put my mum through and she needs me to be here for her. I don't really know what Andy wants. He won't talk, but Becky keeps getting so angry and upset about the situation, I think she might feel like she has to be there for both Mum and Dad, but I don't really see how that can work.

Rebecca: [spoken quietly and sad, with pauses] I hate this…I don't see why it has to be like this, why can't we just go back to how things were?…I want to see my dad, so does Andy…but when we try to speak about it Tasha just doesn't listen, she doesn't understand…I know Mum was sad, but so was Dad…we all were…I don't want to choose between them…why should I?…it's just not fair…

Andrew: [very shy, speaks quietly and softly] I really miss my dad, we are supposed to go camping, but I don't think I'll be able to now. I wish me and Becky could go and stay with him sometime, I don't understand why we can't, but… whenever we talk about it, well, Tasha gets angry and Mum seems sad about it. I don't want to upset anyone, but I need my dad…

Natasha: I still stand by my mum, when you've heard all the fights and banging and smashing that happened here, there's just no reason to bother with my dad, especially now… it kept getting worse and a few weeks ago my mum had a black eye, I know it was him…and that's why I don't want to see him anymore. I hate him, how could he do that to my mum?

Rebecca: I know Tasha is convinced Dad gave Mum the black eye, but I'm not so sure…I've seen Tommy lose his temper and I really don't trust him. I saw my dad yesterday, Mum doesn't know, but he lives near to our school so I went there…I was so happy to see him and he said he really missed us all too. Andy came with me. He wants to take us camping, but if Tasha and Mum find out, then I don't think we'll be able to go.

Andrew: Yeah, me and Becky have seen Dad…after school. We try to go as often as we can, we really miss him. I told Mum I was at chess club…we can't let Tasha know 'cos… well…she really doesn't want us to see him. But Mum said…Mum said that we could if we wanted, it's just it feels like I'm doing something wrong when I want to see him…I don't want to go behind Mum's back, it makes it feel uncomfortable.

Online questionnaire

Parental Separation and Divorce Questionnaire

1. Age

[   ]

2. Gender

○ M

○ F

○ XG

3. Generally, what did you think of the YouTube film clip?

○ It was very realistic

○ It showed some of how I felt when it happened to me

○ It was nothing like I felt in that situation

○ It was how my brother and/or sister responded

○ I don't have an opinion

4. Did you think the case study was realistic?

○ Yes

○ No

5. How old were you when your parents separated?

○ 0 to 4

○ 5 to 8

○ 9 to 12

○ 13 to 16

○ 17 to 20

○ Over 20

6. When you watched the clip, and saw the children's different responses, were there any similarities to your experiences? If so, in what ways?

[   ]

7. When were you told they were going to separate and who told you?

○ As soon as my parents decided to separate

○ A few weeks before one parent left

○ At the time of one parent leaving

○ Found out by overhearing parents arguing

○ Found out after one parent had left

Who told you? [   ]

8. What were your first thoughts and feelings?

[text box]

9. Who did you mainly live with after separation? (please tick)

☐ Other

☐ Mother

☐ Grandparents

☐ Father

☐ Both Equally

Who else lived with you? [   ]

10. Was there a change in the following after separation?

	Yes	No
Living Arrangements	○ Yes	○ No
School	○ Yes	○ No
Adults you Lived With	○ Yes	○ No

Could you explain further... [text box]

11. What immediately changed in your life once you realised your parents were going to separate?

[text box]

12. When these changes happened were your views taken into account? If so, in what way?

[text box]

13. Who was the main source of support for you during these changes?

☐ Mother

☐ Father

☐ Brother(s)

☐ Sister(s)

☐ Grandmother

☐ Grandfather

☐ Aunt

☐ Uncle

☐ Cousin(s)

☐ Friend(s)

☐ No-one

☐ Other

Other (please specify)

14. Can you say more about your thoughts and feelings about these changes at the time?

15. How do you feel about them now?

16. How did other family members respond to these changes? (For example, your mother and father, any brothers and sisters or grandparents).

17. Who did you feel able to talk to about your parents' separation?

☐ Mother

☐ Father

☐ Brother(s)

☐ Sister(s)

☐ Grandmother

☐ Grandfather

☐ Uncle

☐ Aunt

☐ Teacher

☐ Youth Worker

☐ Social Worker

☐ Counsellor

☐ Friend(s)

☐ Other

Other (please specify)

18. Would you have liked the chance to talk to someone outside the family about what was happening? If so, who might that have been? (Remember to identify their role – like Teacher or Youth Worker or Priest - rather than their name)

19. What information would have been useful to you at the time?

20. What advice would you have for a young person whose parents are separating?

Done

Respondent information: identifier number, current age, age at time of separation, gender and level of accommodation

Respondent identifier	Current age	Age at time of separation	Gender	Level of accommodation	Those that lacked continuity
1	18	9–12	Female	Low	
2	27	9–12	Female	Low	
3	19	9–12	Male	High	
4	19	5–8	Female	High	
5	18	9–12	Male	Medium	
6	19	0–4	Female	High	
7	23	0–4	Female	High	
8	20	9–12	Female	High	
9	19	13–16	Female	High	
10	18	9–12	Female	High	
11	20	9–12	Female	High	
12	19	17–20	Female	Low	
13	18	9–12	Male		Lacked continuity
14	20	9–12	Male	High	
15	21	5–8	Female	High	
16	25	5–8	Female	Medium	
17	19	9–12	Female	Low	
18	19	0–4	Female	High	
19	19	13–16	Female	High	
20	30	0–4	Female		Lacked continuity
21	18	9–12	Female	High	
22	25	0–4	Female	Medium	
23	20	5–8	Female	High	
24	27	17–20	Female		Lacked continuity

contnued ...

Respondent identifier	Current age	Age at time of separation	Gender	Level of accommodation	Those that lacked continuity
25	19	5–8	Female	High	
26	19	9–12	Female	High	
27	18	0–4	Female	High	
28	23	9–12	Female	Medium	
29	27	13–16	Male	High	
30	18	0–4	Female	High	
31	19	9–12	Female	High	
32	22	9–12	Male	Medium	
33	30	13–16	Female	Medium	
34	20	17–20	Male		Lacked continuity

APPENDIX FIVE

Table of continua: respondents' positioning according to ID number (34 respondents)

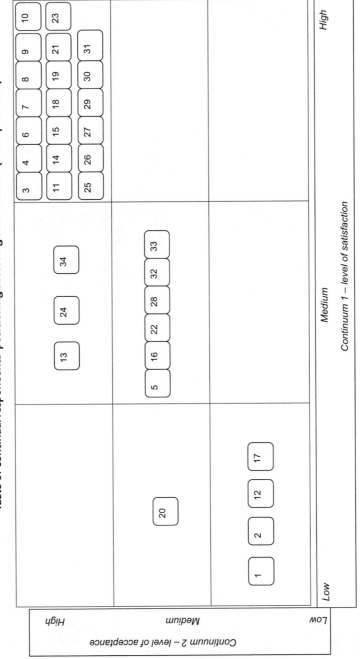

Framework for understanding children's accommodation of parental separation

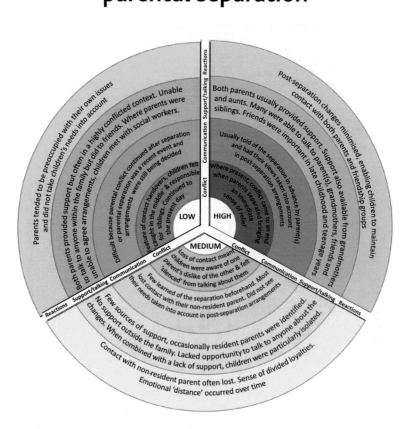

Post-separation changes minimised, enabling children to maintain contact with both parents. Support also available from grandmothers, friends and friendship groups

Both parents usually provided support. Support also available from grandmothers, friends and aunts. Many were able to talk to parent(s), grandmothers, friends and siblings. Friends were important in late childhood and teenage years

Usually told of the separation in advance by parent(s) and had their views taken into account in post-separation arrangements

Where present, conflict came to an end when parents separated bringing an immediate sense of relief

HIGH

LOW

Conflict

Communication Support/talking Reactions

Parents tended to be preoccupied with their own issues and did not take children's needs into account

Both parents provided support but often in a highly conflicted context. Unable to talk to anyone within the family but did to friends. Where parents were unable to agree arrangements, children met with social workers.

Difficult because parental conflict continued after separation or parental separation was a recent event and arrangements were still being decided

Feature of contact handovers, children felt caught in the middle, & responsible for siblings. Continued to the present day

Reactions Support/talking Communication Conflict

MEDIUM Conflict

Loss of contact meant children were aware of one parent's dislike of the other & felt 'silenced' from talking about them

Few learned of the separation beforehand. Most lost contact with their non-resident parent. Did not see their needs taken into account in post-separation arrangements

Few sources of support, occasionally resident parents were identified. No support outside the family. Lacked opportunity to talk to anyone about the changes. When combined with a lack of support, children were particularly isolated.

Contact with non-resident parent often lost. Sense of divided loyalties. Emotional 'distance' occurred over time

Communication Support/talking Reactions

Index

Note: page numbers in *italic* type refer to figures; those in **bold** type refer to tables.

A

Abetz, J. 17, 102, 121, 175
acceptance of parental separation and
    post-separation changes (Continuum
    2) 4, 5, 41, 65, 74
    categorising responses 59, 60, 61, 67, 68
    continuity in 77, **77**
        lack of 78, **78**
    high level 74–6, 80
    low level 74, 77, 80
    medium level 74, 76–7, 80
    table of continua **201**
accommodation of parental separation
    and post-separation changes 4, 41, 42,
    65, 79
    categorising responses 59–61, 67, 68
    continuity in 77, **77**, 79, 80
        lack of 78, **78**
    factors influencing levels of 61–2, 79–80,
        81–2
        children's involvement in decision-
            making 79, 82, 149–51
        communication 79, 80, 84, 149–51
        conflict 79, 80, 81–2, 84–5, 163–4
        contact 81, 82, 84
        friends 81, 83, 84
        reactions 119–21
        support 79, 80, 81, 84, 137
    framework for understanding 67–8
    high level 81, 83, 119–21
    low level 81, 83–4
    medium level 81, 83, 84
    see also acceptance of parental
        separation and post-separation
        changes (Continuum 2); satisfaction
        with parental satisfaction and post-
        separation changes (Continuum 1)
adolescence:
    changes in contact arrangements 27
    and poor parental relationships 30
America 19
anonymity and identity issues in research
    45, 51, 53–4, 63
anxiety 95, 112, 121, 151, 155, 164, 168
    see also mental health issues
Association of Internet Researchers 51
aunts, as source of support 125, **126**, 127,
    129, **130**, 131, 137, 138, 162, 163
Australia 18

B

Bagshaw, D. 17, 18, 19, 21, 27, 32, 33, 34,
    35, 36, 121, 151, 152, 164, 165, 170,
    179
Beausang, J. 17, 33, 164
Belgium 18
Bethany (Respondent 23) 69, 74, 75,
    90–1, 108–9, 125, 128, 130, 131, 138,
    143–4, 145–6, 148, 150, 169
    case study 123–4
Birnbaum, R. 17, 19, 28, 30, 33, 39, 164,
    165
Brand, C. 1, 16, 17, 18, 21, 22, 25, 29, 30,
    33, 36, 37, 121, 138, 171, 179
bricolage 2, 3, 4, 41, 46–7, 62
bricoleur role 4, 46–7, 62
British Educational Research Association,
    Ethical Guidelines 51
Butler, I. 17, 19, 20, 21, 22, 23, 25, 26, 27,
    28, 29, 31, 32, 33, 34, 35, 36, 37, 39,
    101, 121, 138, 151, 165, 170, 171, 174,
    179

C

CAFCASS (Children and Family Court
    Advisory Service) 24, 177
    Family Court Advisors 1–2, 79
CAMHS (Child and Adolescent Mental
    Health Services) 171
Campbell, A. 17, 18, 21, 22, 23–4, 26, 32
Catrina (Respondent 17) 73, 77, 88, 94,
    110, 111, 114, 131, 132, 133, 135, 145,
    149, 157, 158, 163, 164, 165, 168
    case study 153–4
child-centred approach 176, 177
ChildLine 33
children:
    as co-researchers 16
    as 'competent social actors' 15
    number living in cohabiting couple
        families 7, 13–14
    statistics of those affected by divorce
        14–15
        England and Wales **10**, 10–11
        Northern Ireland 11–13, **12**
    UK population statistics 8
    'wishes and feelings' of 2
Children Act 1989 2

Children and Families Act 2014 9, 10
Children and Family Court Advisory
    Service *see* CAFCASS (Children and
    Family Court Advisory Service)
Children's Centres 175
Children's Services 175, 177 , 178
circle time, in schools 33
Civil Partnership Act 2004 8, 12
civil partnerships:
    civil partner couple families, UK
        population statistics 8
    dissolution of 9, 13, **13**
    legislation 7, 8, 13
    Northern Ireland 12–13
    Scotland 13, **13**
cohabiting couple families:
    definition 8
    England and Wales 14
    number of children living in 7, 13–14
    UK population statistics 8, *9*
communication 4, 6, 19–21, 38–9, 68, 80,
    81, 82, 142–3
    case study, Joseph (Respondent 5) 141–2
    children's views not taken into account
        147–9, 150
    impact on level of satisfaction 69
    influence on level of accommodation
        79, 80, 84, 149–51
    involvement in decision-making 21, 120,
        145–9, 150, 151
    learning about separation at time of one
        parent leaving 144–5, 150, 151
    learning about separation in advance
        143–4, 149
    online questionnaire topic 49, 50
conflict 6, 33–5, 68, 80, 81, 82, 154–5,
    164–6, 179
    case study, Catrina (Respondent 17)
        153–4
    exclusion from online questionnaire 49,
        50–1, 63, 154
    family support 162
    and fear 159–60
    impact on emotions 88, 102
    impact on level of satisfaction 72
    influence on level of accommodation
        79, 80, 81–2, 84–5, 163–4
    negative impact on children's social and
        emotional wellbeing 155–8
    post-separation adjustment 161–2
    relief upon ending of 114–15, 158–62,
        165
    see also domestic violence
contact:
    changes in adolescence 27
    children's involvement in decision-
        making 22, 23
    flexibility in 26–7

influence on level of accommodation
    81, 82
judicial decisions 24
late childhood (9–12 years) age group
    111
loss of:
    with fathers 27, 76, 78, 101, 106, 158,
        163, 164, 175
    with non-resident parents 27–8, 37–8,
        82, 83, 84, 114–15, 120–1, 150, 158,
        166
    with siblings 76, 120, 162
    teenage years (13–16 years) age group
        115–16
contact handovers, parental conflict at 34,
    81, 84, 165
content analysis 57–9
    see also data analysis
continuity 4, 24–8
    and acceptance of parental separation
        and post-separation changes
        (Continuum 2) 77, **77**
    and accommodation of parental
        separation and post-separation changes
        77, **77**
    influence on level of accommodation
        79, 80
    lack of, and acceptance of parental
        separation and post-separation changes
        (Continuum 2) 78, **78**
    lack of, and accommodation of parental
        separation and post-separation changes
        78, **78**
    lack of, and satisfaction with, parental
        satisfaction and post-separation
        changes (Continuum 1) 78, **78**
    online questionnaire topic 49
    and satisfaction with parental satisfaction
        and post-separation changes
        (Continuum 1) 77, **77**
    in schools 28
Continuum 1 *see* satisfaction with parental
    satisfaction and post-separation
    changes (Continuum 1)
Continuum 2 *see* acceptance of parental
    separation and post-separation changes
    (Continuum 2)
counsellors, as source of support 129, **130**,
    132, 135, 137, 138, 168, 171
cousins, as source of support 125, **126**,
    128, 138
critical friend 61, 68
Cyr, F. 139

D

data analysis 4, 41, 46–7, 56–7, 67
    categorising responses 59–61
    content analysis 57–9

young people's co-creation of 2

Deater-Deckard, K. 17, 20, 21, 29, 31, 32, 34–5, 121, 138, 165, 179

decision-making, children's involvement in 4, 21, 120
influence on level of accommodation 79, 82, 149–51
online questionnaire topic 49
views being taken into account 145–7
by social workers 149
views not taken into account 147–9

DfE (Department for Education) 172

'diminished parenting' 25, 30, 138

dissolution, of civil partnerships 9, 13, **13**

distance 71, 76
see also emotional distance

divided loyalties 34, 81, 83, 112–13, 115, 121, 163, 165

divorce:
England and Wales 9–11, **10**
legislation 9
Northern Ireland 11–13, **12**
Scotland 13, **13**
statistics 9–13, **10**, **12**, **13**
terminology 3
see also parental separation

Divorce Reform Act 1969 9

domestic violence 24, 50, 81, 84–5, 114, 147, 150, 159–60, 165
see also conflict

Du Plooy, K. 1, 16, 17, 18, 38, 138, 151, 170

Dunn, J. 17, 20, 21, 29, 31, 32, 34–5, 121, 138, 165, 179

E

early years (0–4 years) age group:
emotions, as context for framework 88, **89**, 89–90
reactions 105–8

embarrassment 32–3

Emily (Respondent 12) 73, 77, 98, 99, 118, 126, 127, 131–2, 135, 143, 147, 148–9, 168
case study 87–8, 88–9

emotional burden 34, 166

emotional distance 71, 81, 83, 121, 179

emotional wellbeing of children 170
impact of conflict on 155–8
see also mental health issues

emotions, as context for framework 5, 85, 88–9
case study, Emily (Respondent 12) 87–8
early years (0–4 years) age group 88, **89**, 89–90
late childhood (9–12 years) age group 88, **93**, 93–6, 100, 101

late teenage years (17–20 years) age group 88, 98–100, **99**, 101–2
middle childhood (5–8 years) age group 88, 90–2, **91**, 100, 101
range of 100
teenage years (13–16 years) age group 88, **96**, 96–8, 100, 102

England 7
population statistics 8

England and Wales:
cohabiting couple families 14
divorce 9–11, **10**
female couples' divorce statistics 10
marriage legislation 9
number of children living in stepfamilies 14
parental separation overview 9–11, **10**
same-sex marriage 9, 10
statistics of children affected by divorce **10**, 10–11

ethical issues 51–2

ethnicity, not included in data gathering 64

European Convention on Human Rights 173

extended family members, as source of support 30, 31, 38, 83, 125, **126**, 127–8, **130**, 131, 138

F

Family Court Advisors, CAFCASS 1–2, 79

Family Courts 84, 111, 114, 133, 137, 149, 177

Family Support Centres 175, 178

family types in the UK 7–8, 9

fathers:
behaviour of 27, 159, 163
contact with 26
loss of 27, 76, 78, 101, 106, 158, 163, 164, 175
as source of support 29, 125, 126, **126**, 129, 130, **130**

fear, and parental conflict 159–60

Fehlberg, B. 17, 151, 176

female couples:
civil partnership dissolutions, Northern Ireland 13
divorce statistics, England and Wales 10

Flowerdew, J. 17, 21, 33, 35, 36, 37, 100, 102, 121, 151, 164, 175, 179

focus group 2
and bricolage 46–7
categorising responses 61, 68
composition of 43
discussions 43–4
evaluation 46
research methods 44–5

target audience 45
Fortin, J. 1, 17, 18, 21, 22, 23, 24, 25, 26,
   27–8, 29, 30, 34, 36, 37, 38, 138, 152,
   164, 165, 179
framework for understanding children's
   accommodation of parental separation
   67–8, 178–9, 202
construction of 4, 80–2
future directions for 6, 167–80
understanding of 82–5
value of for families 175–8
value of for practitioners 170–4
   see also communication; conflict;
   reactions; support/talking
friends:
   influence on level of accommodation
   81, 83, 84
   as source of support 31–2, 38, 50, 83,
   124, 125, 126, 128, 129, 130, 131–2,
   137, 138

G

GCSE (General Certificate of Secondary
   Education) exams 36, 97, 100, 121
Gemma (Respondent 22) 68, 71, 72, 76–7,
   89–90, 101, 107, 126, 127, 132, 133,
   134, 135–6, 147, 148, 150 , 154, 156–7,
   163, 168, 175, 176
   case study 103–4, 105
Gingerbread 53, 177
grandchildren, as catalyst for renewed
   contact with non-resident parents in
   adulthood 27, 38
grandparents, as source of support 31, 73,
   83, 92, 94, 103, 107, 108, 113, 125,
   126, 126–7, 130, 130–1, 138, 164
   grandfathers 126, 126, 129, 130, 130–1
   grandmothers 31, 124, 125, 126, 126,
   127, 129, 130, 130–1, 133, 137, 138,
   157

H

Halling, S. 57
Halpenny, A.M. 17, 18, 25, 29, 31, 33, 174
Health Education 173
health issues 97, 168
higher education, respondents in 69, 73,
   74, 78, 87–8, 88–9, 98–9, 100, 107,
   118–19, 121, 130, 132, 135, 147, 168,
   174–5
   support for 167, 174–5
Hogan, D.M. 17, 18, 20, 22, 25, 26, 29, 30,
   31, 32, 34, 35, 37, 151, 152, 165, 174,
   179

I

identity and anonymity issues in research
   45, 51, 53–4, 63

informed consent 52–3
internet:
   as vehicle for research study 44
   see also online questionnaire; PSV
   (prompt simulation video)
Ireland 18, 31
   see also Northern Ireland

J

Joseph (Respondent 5) 71, 76, 88, 93, 95,
   101, 110, 111, 115 , 121, 126, 127, 133,
   135, 144, 147, 148, 150, 151, 154, 158,
   163, 164, 166
   case study 141–2

L

late childhood (9–12 years) age group:
   contact 111
   emotions, as context for framework 88,
   93, 93–6, 100, 101
   reactions 110–15, 120, 121
late teenage years (17–20 years) age group:
   emotions, as context for framework 88,
   98–100, 99, 101–2
   reactions 118–19
legislation 7
   civil partnerships 7, 8, 13
   marriage 7, 9
   see also divorce
lone parent families, UK population
   statistics 8, 9
looking back on childhood experiences
   of parental separation 4, 15, 19, 23, 25,
   37–9
   influence on level of accommodation 79
loss:
   respondents' sense of 72–3, 164
   see also contact, loss of

M

Maes, S.D.J. 17, 18, 20, 22, 28, 120-1 , 139,
   151, 165, 179
Marriage (Same Sex Couples) Act 2013
   9, 10
Marriage and Civil Partnership (Scotland)
   Act 2014 13
marriage legislation 7
   England and Wales 9
married couple families:
   definition 8
   UK population statistics 8, 9
Matrimonial and Family Proceedings Act
   1984 9
Menning, C.L. 17, 18, 27, 30
mental health issues 164, 168
   anxiety 95, 112, 121, 151, 155, 164, 168
   impact of conflict on 155–8
   stress 97, 116–17, 121, 161, 164

see also emotions, as context for
   framework
middle childhood (5–8 years) age group:
   emotions, as context for framework 88,
      90–2, **91**, 100, 101
   reactions 108–10, 120
Morrison, S.C. 1, 16, 17, 18, 19, 38–9, 138,
      151, 175, 176, 179
mothers, as source of support 29, 125, 126,
      126, 129, 130, **130**
Moxnes, K. 17, 18, 21, 22, 23, 25, 27, 28,
      29, 30, 34, 35, 36, 139, 151, 152, 164,
      165, 179
'multiple transitions' 17, 21, 151

N

Neale, B. 17, 21, 33, 35, 36, 37, 100, 102,
      121, 151, 164, 175, 179
New Zealand 18
NISRA (Northern Ireland Statistics and
      Research Agency) 11–13, **12**
no one, support from 124, 125, **126**, 129,
      130, 133–4, 163–4
non-resident parents:
   children's resentment of demands by
      30, 34
   contact with 26–7, 108, 120, 150
      loss of 27–8, 37–8, 82, 83, 84, 114–15,
         120–1, 150, 158, 166
   impact on emotions 88
   impact on reactions 121
   influence on level of accommodation 84
   and level of satisfaction 71
   renewed contact in adulthood 27–8, 38,
      177–8
non-resident step-parents 36
Northern Ireland 7
   civil partnerships 12–13
   divorce 11–13, **12**
   female couples' civil partnership
      dissolutions 13
   non-recognition of same-sex marriage
      12
   parental separation overview 11–13, **12**
   population statistics 8
   statistics of children affected by divorce
      11–13, **12**
   see also Ireland
Northern Ireland Statistics and Research
      Agency (NISRA) 11–13, **12**
Norway 18

O

online questionnaire 2, 41, 44–5, 63
   construction 48
   content 49–51
   copy of 195–8
   ethical issues 51–2

exclusion of conflict from 49, 50–1, 63,
      154
   focus group involvement 51
   identity and anonymity issues 53–4
   informed consent 52–3
   pilot study 54–5
   sources of support 52, 53

P

parental communication *see*
      communication
parental conflict *see* conflict
parental separation overview:
   England and Wales 9–11, **10**
   Northern Ireland 11–13, **12**
   Scotland 13, **13**
   terminology 3
parental support *see* support/talking
'parenting coordination', Canada 139
'Parenting Plan, The' 177
parents:
   'diminished parenting' 25, 30, 138
   good relationships with 25–7
   as source of support 28–3 0, 38–9, 124,
      125–6, **126**, 130, **130**, 137, 138, 167–8,
      179
   fathers 29, 125, 126, **126**, 129, 130, **130**
   mothers 29, 125, 126, **126**, 129, 130,
      130
   value of framework for understanding
      children's accommodation of parental
      separation for 175–8
   see also communication; conflict; fathers;
      non-resident parents; resident parent;
      step-parents
peer support 33, 167, 171, 174–5
Personal, Social and Health Education
      (PSHE) 33, 167, 169, 171–4
pilot study 54–5
   see also research study
population statistics, UK 7–8
post-separation arrangements:
   adjustment to 161–2
   children's involvement in decision-
      making 21, 22–3, 49, 79, 82, 120,
      145–9, 149–51
   children's unhappiness with 20
   judicial decisions 23, 24, 84, 111, 114,
      133, 137, 149, 177
post-separation family transitions 4
   children's experiences of 35–7
   influence on level of accommodation 79
   timing of 36–7
practitioners, value of framework for 167,
      170–4, 178
primary schools:
   primary-secondary transition 101, 155,
      168

Relationships Education 172–3
professionals, as source of support 125,
    128–9, **130**, 132–3, 135, 138
prompt simulation video *see* PSV (prompt
    simulation video)
PSHE (Personal, Social and Health
    Education) 33, 167, 169, 171–4
PSV (prompt simulation video) 2, 4, 41,
    46, 47, 62, 63, 103, 104–5, 107, 112
    actors' script 192–4
    case study 189–91
    dramatisation 47
    filming 48
    identity and anonymity issues 53–4
    parental conflict 50–1
    pilot study 54
'psychological travelling time' 35, 36, 121
psychologists, as source of support 171

Q

qualitative research 3
Quigley, C. 139

R

Rainbows programme 31, 173, 174
re-partnering:
    number and timing of 35, 36
    same-sex 37
    see also step-parents
reactions 5, 68, 80, 81, 82, 83, 104–5, 121
    case study, Gemma (Respondent 22)
        103–4, 105
    early years (0–4 years) age group 105–7
    higher levels of accommodation where
        changes were minimised 119–21
    late childhood (9–12 years) age group
        110–15, 120, 121
    late teenage years (17–20 years) age
        group 118–19
    middle childhood (5–8 years) age group
        108–10, 120
    teenage years (13–16 years) age group
        115–17, 120
reconciliation 70
Relate 177
Relationships and Sex Education,
    secondary schools 172–4
Relationships Education, primary schools
    172–3
relief, sense of 114–15, 119, 158–62, 165
research study 41 –65
    aims of 41, 42
    bricolage 2, 3, 4, 41, 46–7, 62
    data analysis 2, 4, 6–47, 56–61, 67
    focus group 2, 43–7, 61, 68
    identity and anonymity 53–4
    limitations of 41, 64–5
    main study 55–6, *56*

pilot study 54–5
reflections on methodology 41, 62–4
target audience 45
young people's co-creation of design 2,
    3, 4, 40, 41, 42–53, 62
    see also online questionnaire; PSV
    (prompt simulation video); research
    tools
research tools:
    reflection on 62–4
    young people's co-creation of 2, 3, 4, 40,
        41, 44–5
    see also online questionnaire; PSV
    (prompt simulation video)
residence arrangements 109
    children's involvement in decision-
        making 23, 24
    continuity in 28
    judicial decisions 24
    online questionnaire topic 49, 50
resident parents:
    difficulties in coping with separation
        29–30
    as source of support 29, 81, 83, 126, 138,
        168
    see also parents
resident step-parents 23, 35–6, 155
Respondent 1 73, 77, 88, 93, 94, 110, 111,
    114, 131, 132, 133, 135, 139, 145, 149,
    154, 157–8, 163, 164, 165, 168
Respondent 2 73, 77, 93, 94, 101, 110,
    113, 115, 129, 133, 134, 145, 154, 163,
    164, 168
Respondent 3 69, 71, 74, 93, 95, 110, 112,
    115, 126, 127, 128, 130, 131, 136
Respondent 4 69, 74, 75, 90, 91, 108,
    109–10, 129, 133, 134, 145, 147, 148
Respondent 5 (Joseph) 71, 76, 88, 93, 95,
    101, 110, 111, 114, 121, 126, 127, 133,
    135, 144, 147, 148, 150, 151, 154, 158,
    163, 164, 166
    case study 141–2
Respondent 6 69, 74.89, 105, 126, 128,
    130, 131, 143, 145
Respondent 7 69, 71, 74, 89, 105–6, 126,
    127, 132, 133, 145, 168
Respondent 8 69, 70, 74, 93, 110, 126,
    127, 128, 130, 131, 132–3, 143, 145
Respondent 9 69, 74, 75, 96, 97–8,
    115–16, 117, 128, 131–2, 136, 143,
    144, 145–6, 149, 150, 154, 156, 162,
    163, 166
Respondent 10 69, 74, 88, 93, 96, 114,
    126, 127, 130, 136, 143, 144, 147, 150,
    151, 154, 159, 160, 163, 165, 169
Respondent 11 69, 74, 75, 93, 95, 101,
    110, 112, 115, 129, 131, 136, 145–6,
    150, 154, 155, 163, 164, 168

Respondent 12 (Emily) 73, 77, 98, 99,
    118, 126, 127, 131–2, 135, 143, 147,
    148–9, 168
  case study 87–8, 88–9
Respondent 13 71, 74, 78, 93, 95, 96, 101,
    107, 111, 114, 120, 121, 126, 128, 130,
    135, 144, 147, 148, 151, 164
Respondent 14 69, 71, 74, 93, 95, 110,
    112, 115, 126, 127, 128, 130, 131, 136,
    144, 145–6, 150
Respondent 15 69, 70, 74, 90, 91, 108,
    109, 129, 133, 134, 145, 147
Respondent 16 71–2, 76, 90, 91, 92, 101,
    108, 110, 129, 133, 134, 144
Respondent 17 (Catrina) 73, 77, 88, 94,
    110, 111, 114, 131, 132, 133, 135, 145,
    149, 157, 158, 163, 164, 165, 168
  case study 153–4
Respondent 18 69, 74, 89, 105, 126, 128,
    130, 131, 136, 143, 145
Respondent 19 69, 70, 74, 96, 97, 98, 115,
    117, 128, 143, 144, 145–6, 150, 154,
    155–6, 163
Respondent 20 73, 76, 78, 89, 105, 106,
    107, 120, 121, 143, 175–6
Respondent 21 69, 74, 88, 93, 96, 110,
    114, 126, 127, 130, 136, 143, 145–6,
    147, 150, 151, 154, 159–60, 163, 165,
    169
Respondent 22 (Gemma) 68, 71, 72, 76–7,
    89–90, 101, 107, 126, 127, 132, 133,
    134, 135–6, 147, 148, 150, 154 , 156–7,
    163, 168, 175, 176
  case study 103–4, 105
Respondent 23 (Bethany) 69, 74, 75,
    90–1, 108–9, 125, 128, 130, 131, 138,
    143–4, 145–6 , 150, 169
  case study 123–4
Respondent 24 71, 72, 74, 78, 98, 99–100,
    118, 119, 120, 121, 130, 134, 135, 143,
    144, 154, 158–9, 163, 168, 169
Respondent 25 69, 70, 74, 90, 91–2, 108,
    109, 126, 127, 128, 130, 131, 136, 144,
    145–6, 150, 154, 161, 163, 165, 180
Respondent 26 69, 70, 74, 93, 110,
    112–13, 115, 126, 127, 128, 130, 131,
    132–3, 143, 145
Respondent 27 69 , 74, 76, 89, 105, 106,
    130, 136, 145
Respondent 28 71 , 76, 88, 93, 96, 110,
    113, 115, 120, 133–4, 143, 144, 145–6,
    147, 150 , 154, 161–2, 163, 164, 166,
    168
Respondent 29 68, 69, 70, 74, 96, 98, 115,
    116, 117, 120, 121, 128–9, 132, 133,
    136, 147, 148, 175
Respondent 30 69, 71, 74, 89, 105, 106–7,
    120, 126, 127, 130, 131

Respondent 31 69 , 74, 75, 79, 88, 93, 94,
    110, 112, 115, 129, 131, 136, 145–6,
    147, 150, 151, 154, 155, 163, 168
Respondent 32 71, 76, 93, 95, 101, 110,
    111, 114, 121, 127, 136, 144, 147, 148,
    150
Respondent 33 71, 76, 96, 97, 115,
    116–17, 120, 121, 129, 133, 143, 144,
    145–6, 147, 150, 168, 169
Respondent 34 71, 74–5, 78, 98, 99,
    118–19, 130, 131, 132, 144, 147, 169
respondents 41, 63
  age at parental separation 55–6, 57
  age profile 55, 56, 63
  continua, table of **201**
  elapsed time since parental separation
    56, 58, 71
  gender profile 55, 63
  identity and anonymity 45, 51, 53–4, 63
  informed consent 52–3
  main study 55–6
  pilot study 54–5
  profile of 199–200
romantic partners, as source of support 38

S

Saini, M. 17, 19, 28, 30, 33, 39, 164, 165
Samaritans 53
same-sex families, not identifiable in
    research study 64
same-sex marriage:
  England and Wales 9, 10
  non-recognition of in Northern Ireland
    12
  Scotland 13
same-sex re-partnering 37
satisfaction with parental satisfaction and
    post-separation changes (Continuum
    1) 4, 5, 41, 65
  categorising responses 60, 61, 67, 68
  continuity in 77, **77**
    lack of 78, **78**
  high level 69–71
  impact of communication on 69
  influence of contact with non-resident
    parents 71
  low level 69, 72–3
  medium level 69, 71–2
  table of continua **201**
schools:
  circle time 33
  continuity in 28
  primary-secondary transition 101, 155,
    168
  sex education 171–4
  as source of support 32–33, 168–74
  see also PSHE (Personal, Social and
    Health Education)

Scotland 7
    civil partnerships 13, **13**
    divorce 13, **13**
    parental separation overview 13, **13**
    population statistics 8
    same-sex marriage 13
secondary schools:
    primary-secondary transition 101, 155, 168
    Relationships and Sex Education 172–4
SENCos (Special Educational Needs Co-ordinators), pastoral staff supporting 170–1
Separating Parents Information Programme (SPIP) 177
Sex and Relationship Education (SRE) 171–2, 176
sex education 171–4
sexual identity of children 37
shame 32–3
siblings:
    loss of contact with 76, 120, 162
    responsibility for 30, 84, 161
    as source of support 31, 125, **126**, 128, 129, **130**, 131, 138
Smart, C. 17, 18, 23, 24, 26, 27, 29, 30, 31, 33, 34, 35, 37, 39, 121, 165, 170, 171, 174, 176, 179
Smith, A.B. 17, 18, 21, 22, 23, 24, 25, 26, 34, 151, 152, 164, 165, 179
social wellbeing of children, impact of conflict on 155–8
social workers 166
    children's views taken into account by 149
    as source of support 84, 129, 132, 133, 135, 137, 138, 171
South Africa 18
Special Educational Needs Co-ordinators (SENCos), pastoral staff supporting 170–1
SPIP (Separating Parents Information Programme) 177
spiritual beliefs, as source of support 38
SRE (Sex and Relationship Education) 171–2, 176
step-parents 155
    children's involvement in decision-making 23
    introduction of 35–6
    number of children living in stepfamilies, England and Wales 14
    resident 23, 35–6, 155
    stepfathers 35–6
stress 97, 121, 161, 164
    teenage years (13–16 years) age group 116–17

support/talking 5–6, 32–33, 68, 80, 81, 82, 83–84, 124–5, **126**, 129–36, **130**, 137–9, 167–8
    aunts 125, **126**, 127, 129, **130**, 131, 137, 138, 162, 163
    case study, Bethany (Respondent 23) 123–4, 125
    and conflict 162, 163, 166
    counsellors 129, **130**, 132, 135, 137, 138, 168, 171
    cousins 125, **126**, 128, 138
    extended family members 30, 31, 38, 83, 125, **126**, 127–8, **130**, 131, 138
    fathers 29, 125, 126, **126**, 129, 130, **130**
    formal sources 33
    friends 31–2, 38, 50, 83, 124, 125, **126**, 128, 129, **130**, 131–2, 137, 138
    grandparents 31, 73, 83, 92, 94, 103, 107, 108, 113, 125, **126**, 126–7, **130**, 130–1, 138, 164
        grandfathers 126, **126**, 129, **130**, 130–1
        grandmothers 31, 124, 125, 126, **126**, 127, 129, **130**, 130–1, 133, 137, 138, 157
    influence on level of accommodation 79, 80, 81, 84, 137
    mothers 29, 125, 126, **126**, 129, 130, **130**
    no one 124, 125, **126**, 129, **130**, 133–4, 163–4
    online questionnaire topic 49, 50, 52, 53
    parents 28–3 0, 38–9, 124, 125–6, **126**, 130, **130**, 137, 138, 167–8, 179
        resident parents 29, 81, 83, 126, 138, 168
    professionals 125, 128–9, **130**, 132–3, 135, 138
    psychologists 171
    romantic partners 38
    schools 32–3, 168, 170–4
    siblings 31, 125, **126**, 128, 129, **130**, 131, 138
    social workers 84, 129, 132, 133, 135, 137, 138, 171
    spiritual beliefs 38
    uncles 125, **126**, 128, 129, **130**, 131, 138
    views on opportunity to talk to someone 134–6
    youth club leaders 125, 133
    youth workers 129, **130**, 132, 135, 137, 138, 168
Survey Monkey 48, 57
    see also online questionnaire

T

talking to others *see* support/talking
target audience for research study 45
teachers *see* schools
teenage years (13–16 years) age group:

contact 115–16
emotions, as context for framework 88,
  96, 96–8, 100, 102
reactions 115–17, 120
stress 116–17
'torn' feeling 71, 115
transitions:
  post-separation family transitions 4,
    35–7, 79
  primary-secondary education transition
    101, 155, 168
two-household living 24–5
  and children's involvement in decision-
    making 21

U

UK, population statistics 7–8
uncles, as source of support 125, **126**, 128,
  129, **130**, 131, 138
university, respondents at 73, 74, 78, 87–8,
  88–9, 98–9, 100, 107, 118–19, 121,
  130, 132, 135, 147, 168, 174–5
  support for 167, 174–5

V

Van Rensburg, E. 1, 16, 17, 18, 38, 138,
  151, 170
'voice', of children 1, 2
  challenges in accessing/parental
    mediation of 14–15, 39
  importance of 7, 15–16
  relevant studies 16–40
'voice', of young adults 1, 3, 15, 39–40,
  62–3, 178–80

W

Wade, A. 17, 23, 24, 26, 27, 29, 32, 33, 39,
  121, 170, 171, 174
Wales 7, 8
  see also England and Wales
Wang, T.R. 17, 102, 121, 175
'wishes and feelings' of children 2

Y

young adults:
  childhood experiences of parental
    conflict 34
  co-creation of research study 2, 3, 4, 40,
    41, 42–53, 62
  co-creation of research tools 2, 3, 4, 40,
    41, 44–5
  relevant studies on reflection on
    childhood experiences of parental
    separation 37–9
  see also 'voice', of young adults
Young Minds 53
Young People's Advisory Service 53

youth club leaders, as source of support
  125, 133
youth clubs/centres 175
youth workers, as source of support 129,
  130, 132, 135, 137, 138, 168
YouTube website:
  as vehicle for research study 44, 45
  see also PSV (prompt simulation video)